Building Integrated Markets within
the East African Community

A WORLD BANK STUDY

Building Integrated Markets within the East African Community

EAC Opportunities in Public-Private Partnership Approaches to the Region's Infrastructure Needs

THE WORLD BANK
Washington, D.C.

Contents

Appendices

Boxes

Figures

Maps

Tables

Foreword

East Africa is one of the fastest growing economic regions in the world. Partner States of the East African Community (EAC) recognize the significance of infrastructure development if this growth trajectory is to be maintained and strengthened and is to provide a balanced distribution of benefits across the community. The EAC Secretariat is committed to supporting its Partner States in this objective through the development of an integrated dynamic regional economy built on a backbone of robust infrastructure that provides efficient services that advance the competitiveness of the region within the wider global economy. Given the substantial investment sums assessed to be required across the key energy, transport, and water sectors, the Secretariat recognized the importance of attracting private sector investment and expertise to contribute to this objective.

To this end, in 2010, the East African Community Secretariat approached the World Bank to assist the East African Community in undertaking a diagnostic study into the ways and means by which the EAC—its Secretariat, associated entities, and Partner States—could better foster regional public-private partnership (PPP) projects. With the additional financing support of Trademark East Africa, an extensive dialogue and consultative process was launched with a core World Bank technical team to assess current PPP enabling environment conditions across the community and identify actions that could be taken to augment the attractiveness of the regional PPP market for private investment in key sectors and projects.

This report is the welcome outcome of this two-year intensively dialogued exercise. With the approval and adoption of the report at the EAC 28th Ordinary Meeting of its Council of Ministers, the Secretariat looks forward to its further involvement with Partner States to implement its key recommendations.

Dr. Enos S. Bukuku
Deputy Secretary General
Planning and Infrastructure
East African Community Secretariat

Acknowledgments

This report has been prepared by a team from the World Bank Group led by Peter Mousley from the African Region Finance and Private Sector Department and Clive Harris from the World Bank Institute, together with Victoria Rigby-Delmon from the World Bank Private Sector Development Legal Department. The other principal World Bank Group contributors to the report are Evans Osano on capital markets, Zachary Kaplan on public-private partnership (PPP) policy and pipeline issues, Paul Murgatroyd on the East African Development Bank, and Edmund Crawley and Agnieszka Lyniewska, both on East African Community (EAC) Partner State PPP frameworks and portfolios. Case studies were prepared by Anil Bhandari (Kenya-Uganda Railway), James Leigland (Mozambique to South Africa Toll Road), and Samuel Mensah (West Africa Gas Pipeline). Written comments on earlier drafts were received from the following colleagues: Raymond Bordeaux, Vickram Cutteree, Michael Opagi and team, and Michel Noel. Feedback was also provided by Irina Astrakhan, Yusupha Crooks, Michael Fuchs, and Paul Noumba. Additional editorial work on the final report was done by Amy Gautem.

The report is a culmination of diagnostic work and consultations done in close cooperation with the East African Community Secretariat, the East African Development Bank, and key representatives from Partner States via country consultations and through a World Bank Institute–hosted Technical (Nairobi August 2011) and EAC Secretariat–hosted Experts (October 2011) and Validation (July 2012) Workshops. The World Bank team expresses its sincere thanks to the wide range of counterparts from the East Africa region who gave their time and expertise to this exercise.

The authors particularly extend thanks to Dr. Enos Bukuku, Deputy Secretary General, Planning and Infrastructure at the East African Community Secretariat, and his colleagues, Director Tharcisse Kadede and Frederick Owiti, Private Sector Development Officer, for their continued support and technical and other guidance provided over the course of this diagnostic and consultative initiative. Their deep knowledge of the region and understanding of the EAC was fundamental to the success of this endeavor. The authors also especially acknowledge Trademark East Africa for its financial support to this exercise and in particular Director George Wolf and Scott Allen, Deputy CEO, for their sustained personal commitment and technical advice on the report.

Abbreviations

AADFI	Association of African Development Finance Institutions
AfDB	African Development Bank
ALL	América Latina Logística
ANC	African National Congress
ANE	Administracao Nacional de Estradas
BLT	build-lease-transfer
BOO	build, own, operate
BOOT	build-own-operate-transfer
BOT	build-operate-transfer
BROT	build-rehabilitate-operate-transfer
CAA	Conceded Assets Account
CABEI	Central American Bank for Economic Integration
CCTTFA	Central Corridor Transit Transport Facilitation Agency
CEB	Communauté Electrique du Bénin
CEO	chief executive officer
CNL	Chevron Nigeria Limited
CPI	consumer price index
CSIR	Council for Scientific and Industrial Research
DB	design/build
DBSA	Development Bank of South Africa
DEG	German Development Finance Corporation
DFI	Development Finance Institution
DFRC	Development Finance Resource Center
DOT	Department of Transport
DRC	Democratic Republic of Congo
DSG	Deputy Secretary General (ECA)
DTI	Department of Trade and Industry
EAC	East African Community
EACDF	East African Community Development Fund

http://dx.doi.org/10.1596/978-1-4648-0227-0

EADB	East African Development Bank
EARH	East African Railways and Harbors
EASRA	East African Member States Securities Regulatory Authorities
ECOWAS	Economic Community of West African States
EIA	Environmental Impact Assessment
EIB	European Investment Bank
ELPS	Escravos-Lagos Pipeline System
EMP	environmental management plan
EOI	expressions of interest
EPEC	European PPP Expertise Center
ERA	Electricity Regulatory Authority
EU	European Union
EWURA	Energy and Water Utilities Regulatory Authority Act
FIL	Financial Intermediary Loan
FMO	Netherlands Development Finance Company
GDP	gross domestic product
GIZ	Deutsche Gesellschaft für Internationale Zusammenarbeit
GoK	Government of Kenya
GoU	Government of Uganda
GSA	Gas Sales Agreement
GTA	Gas Transportation Agreement
IA	Implementing Authority
ICT	information and communication technology
IDA	International Development Association
IDP	Institutional Development Program
IFC	International Finance Corporation
IGAD	Intergovernmental Authority on Development
IOSCO	International Organization of Securities Commissions
IPA	International Project Agreement
IPP	Independent Power Producers
IPSC	Inter-Ministerial PPP Steering Committee (Rwanda)
KfW	Kreditanstalt für Wiederaufbau
KPLC	Kenya Power and Lighting Company
KRC-URC	Kenya-Uganda Railway
KURH	Kenya Uganda Railway Holdings
LCDFF	Local Currency Debt Financing Facility
LRO	lease-rehabilitate-operate
LVBC	Lake Victoria Basin Commission
MCC	Maputo Corridor Company

MDA	ministries, departments, and agencies
MDC	Maputo Development Corridor
MIGA	Multilateral Investment Guarantee Agency
MMBtu	million metric British thermal units
MMcfd	millions of cubic feet per day
MoF	Ministry of Finance
MoU	memorandum of understanding
MRC	Magadi Railway Company
MSATR	Mozambique-South Africa Toll Road
MW	megawatts
NCCA	Northern Corridor Coordination Authority
NEPAD	New Partnership for Africa's Development
NGC	Nigerian Gas Company
NNPC	Nigerian National Petroleum Corporation
NPL	nonperforming loans
NWSC	National Water and Sewerage Corporation
OPIC	Overseas Private Investment Corporation, U.S.A.
PDF	Project Development Facility
PMO	Prime Minister's Office
PPD	Public-Private Dialogue (Burundi)
PPDA	Public Procurement and Disposal of Public Assets
PPI Database	Private Participation in Infrastructure Project Database
PPIAF	Public-Private Infrastructure Advisory Facility
PPP	public-private partnership
PPPC	Public Private Partnership Committee
PPRA	Public Procurement Regulatory Authority
PRG	Partial Risk Guarantee
PRI	Political Risk Insurance
PSD	private sector development
RAP	resettlement action plan
REC	Regional Economic Community
ROT	rehabilitate-operate-transfer
RPPA	Rwanda Public Procurement Authority
RVR	Rift Valley Railway
SADC	Southern African Development Community
SBB	Stocks and Stocks, Basil Read and Bouygues
SBP	Strategic Business Plan
SCEP	Service Charge des Enterprises Publiques (Burundi)
SDI	Spatial Development Initiative

Building Integrated Markets within the East African Community
http://dx.doi.org/10.1596/978-1-4648-0227-0

SoBeGaz	Société Beninoise de Gaz S.A.
SOE	state-owned enterprise
SoToGaz	Société Togolaise de Gaz S.A.
SPDC	Shell Petroleum Development Corporation of Nigeria Limited
SWOT	Strengths, Weaknesses, Opportunities and Threats
TANESCO	Tanzania Electric Supply Company Limited
TIC	Tanzanian Investment Centre
TMEA	Trademark East Africa
TRAC	Trans Africa Concessions consortium
URC	Uganda Railways Corporation
USAID	United States Agency for International Development
VfM	value for money
VGF	Viability Gap Facility
Vpd	vehicles per day
VRA	Volta River Authority
WAGP	West African Gas Pipeline
WAGPA	West African Gas Pipeline Authority
WAGPCo	West African Gas Pipeline Company
WAPP	West African Power Pool
WB	World Bank
WBI	World Bank Institute

Executive Summary

Background

There are significant economic gains to be realized if the East Africa subregion improves the overall integration of its markets. But infrastructure development that links markets across countries faces particular challenges—political, institutional, and economic. In the case of East Africa, these challenges have served to hold back investment into regional infrastructure, despite significant recent efforts within the region to develop regional infrastructure investment plans and promote an increased use of Public-Private Partnership (PPP) approaches to mobilize private sector financing and expertise.

The East African Community (EAC) Secretariat sought, in collaboration with its Partner States, the World Bank (WB) and Trademark East Africa (TMEA), to (i) review the current enabling status for PPPs in terms of the policy and regulatory framework at the national and EAC levels and the financing environment; (ii) assess, via case studies, other regional PPP initiatives for lessons learned; and (iii) identify options for the development of a framework for PPPs at the EAC level encompassing a regional policy framework, a center of PPP expertise at the EAC level, and financing interventions. Based on this diagnostic, the Secretariat plans to develop a strategy for implementing the approved recommendations.

All EAC Partner States have recognized the role that PPPs can play in helping to provide infrastructure and services in the region. They are all taking active measures to improve their PPP frameworks and all but Burundi have passed or are in the process of passing specific PPP legislation. More than 80 PPP projects have already reached financial close in the region, with the main sectors being telecommunications and power. At the same time, experiences have been mixed with some PPPs and the Partner States are all seeking to strengthen frameworks for PPPs and to build capacity to identify, prepare, negotiate, and implement PPPs more effectively.

There are substantial challenges to scaling up the role PPPs can play in meeting basic service needs in the EAC. These include the small size of domestic PPP markets; limited existing capacities in the public sector; negative perceptions among stakeholders regarding PPPs; a lack of a coordination mechanism to deal with regional PPPs; and financing gaps at the national and regional levels. However, it is clear that whatever actions the EAC takes must complement activities under way at the national levels of the Partner States, rather than cut across them.

Core Recommendations of the Report

On policy framework, strategy, and establishment of a task force: Building on the guidance received to date from the different consultative phases of this diagnostic exercise, from the initial scoping mission through the Experts' Workshop held in October 2011, the Partner State Consultations concluded in May 2012, and the July 2012 Validation Workshop, this report recommends that:

- The EAC create a **Policy Framework** for regional PPPs
- This framework be linked to a **Strategic Business Plan** (SBP) developed to give effect to this policy through a targeted effort to develop and bring to market two to three "regional" projects to demonstrate that such projects can be successful in the region
- The EAC Secretariat and its Partner States establish a **Task Force** that would provide the operational and technical delivery team and initial financial resources for the EAC to develop and mobilize actions needed to implement the SBP.

The policy framework should provide a definition of a regional PPP that will be used to determine eligibility for selection and development of regional projects. It is recommended that this definition cover both cross-border projects and projects that are geographically contained in one state but have significant influence on others. In the latter case, a state may choose to develop such a PPP as a domestic project even if it satisfies this definition. The policy framework should, at least initially, confine coverage to the power, transport, water, and information and communication technology (ICT) sectors. It could create a mechanism for sharing experience in project development, marketing the EAC as a common investment destination, developing expertise at a regional level, and finding regional solutions to the lack of long-term financing.

The two key elements recommended for the proposed framework center on:

- **A Regional Resource Center:** It is recommended that the resource center be located in the East African Development Bank (EADB), given the need to have a focus on practical aspects related to the preparation and financing of PPPs. The resource center could have a number of functions. It will be necessary to be selective, at least initially, as not all functions should be initiated at the same time, but rather evolve gradually, as demand and absorptive capacity develop. Functions include (i) training and knowledge exchange; (ii) convergence of PPP approaches; (iii) regional PPP coordination; (iv) engagement with private sector and other stakeholders; and (v) advisory services. The

EADB is seen as the best place to locate this due to the skills available there from related activities and the need for a practical center rather than an academic one. A full resource center would require at least three qualified professionals and a significant budget. A more streamlined option is recommended initially, with one full-time staff member who will assist an associated task force in fulfilling its terms of reference and developing its capabilities;

- **Financing Instruments:** The report also recommends funding options for regional PPPs. The two main products identified are a Viability Gap Facility (VGF), which would bridge the gap between the commercial viability of a regional PPP and its economic viability; and a Project Development Facility (PDF), which could support the preparation costs of regional PPPs. The VGF could potentially be linked to the EAC Development Fund. Partner States need to be aware when designing these products that they may compete for funds with domestic financing needs. The report also considers the desirability of a regional long-term debt facility, and while there is widespread recognition of the need for longer-term local currency financing, the challenges involved in implementing such a facility are such that this will need to be revisited at a future date.

CHAPTER 1

The Status of PPP Frameworks and Portfolios in the EAC

Background

The Partner States of the East African Community (EAC) recognize the important role that infrastructure development has on the future of the region. In his maiden speech on May 10, 2011, the Secretary General of the EAC emphasized infrastructure development as one of the five priorities for his term in office and stated that the "EAC was working with various partners to actualize Public-Private Partnerships (PPPs) as a financing option for key infrastructure projects in the region."

The importance of efficient infrastructure stock to economic growth is increasingly recognized. The 2008 Commission on Growth and Development in its "Growth Report" (Commission on Growth and Development 2008, 35) noted that:

> In fast growing Asia, public investment in infrastructure accounts for 5–7% of GDP or more. In China, Thailand, and Vietnam total infrastructure investment exceeds 7 percent of GDP. History suggests this is the right order of magnitude for high and sustained growth, although it is difficult to be precise.

The report goes on to highlight the importance of infrastructure development as a key means to increase investment opportunities across other sectors of the economy. Specifically in the case of Africa, the report highlights the importance of infrastructure to the evolution of a more connected continental market—an objective at the heart of the EAC mandate. However, while the EAC subregion has been registering some of the most robust growth levels worldwide—for instance, 2011 saw an average growth rate for the region of 5.8 percent, with an annual average from 2000 to 2009 of 6.1 percent—investment in infrastructure has been more modest, with average levels of public capital expenditures in the infrastructure sectors over the period 2001–06 amounting to 4.8 percent in Uganda, 2.32 percent in Kenya, 2.2 percent in Rwanda, and 1.5 percent in Tanzania (Africa Infrastructure Country Diagnostics [AICD] 2008).[1]

Much of the infrastructure requirements of the region demand cross-country coordination and harmonization. In a key EAC "Corridor Diagnostic Report" for the Northern and Central Corridors, the projected cost of meeting the transport infrastructure needs alone in the EAC for the next five years is US$4.2 billion (East African Community [EAC] 2011). It is estimated that only a portion of this can be met through national budgets and would require very significant increases relative to the average levels of public investment in new capital stock over the 2001–06 period as referenced above. Moreover, while much of the estimated capital investment requirements in these corridors are located in specific EAC Partner States, in some cases the need is for cross-border infrastructure or infrastructure located in one state with the benefits significantly accruing to another. This is the case, for instance, with port development, where landlocked EAC states have specific entrepôt[2] requirements at coastal country ports. Where national funding is scarce, this can pose difficult political choices. In these cases, optimal investment decisions require a regional rather than a national strategic approach. This is where a longer-term, more regionally integrated approach to appraisal and decision making is particularly valuable. This is also where the role of the EAC in supporting a more regional strategic approach could be most constructive. There is also a need to determine how and where to mobilize additional sources of infrastructure financing. It is from this context that the EAC Secretariat has been investigating ways and means to further develop the regional infrastructure market for PPPs.

The Partner States recognize the importance of finding new sources of finance for these projects, including involvement of the private sector and PPPs. The Partner States also recognize that involving the private sector in infrastructure and service delivery can bring a number of benefits, such as efficiency and technology, and can stimulate the development of local expertise and knowledge transfer. The Corridor Diagnostic Report suggests that of the 28 priority projects listed for the two corridors, 22 have potential for some private investment. As described in more detail in chapter 2, each of the Partner States is committed to providing an enabling environment for PPP projects. They are strengthening their legal and institutional frameworks and public sector capabilities to more effectively implement PPP projects. However, there is recognition that PPPs are complex and difficult to get right and that the private sector will be reluctant to invest in PPPs unless they are confident that there is a clear enabling environment and strong commitment from government.

Collectively, the Partner States have a relatively long experience with PPPs, including private participation in the telecoms, transport, and power sectors, commencing in the mid-1990s. However, some mixed experiences has hindered the evolution of the PPP market in the subregion, although there has been a more recent growing recognition of the potential role that PPP structures can play in helping to fill the infrastructure needs in their respective countries. As a result, Partner States are all now taking measures to strengthen their PPP frameworks. This section reviews current steps being taken to develop these frameworks as well as country-level PPP portfolios.

Partner State PPP Frameworks

Four of the EAC Partner States (Kenya, Tanzania, Rwanda, and Uganda) have issued PPP policies and/or have passed PPP bills or are in the process of doing so. Burundi has drafted a law under the auspices of a Public-Private Dialogue Secretariat that takes the lead on the PPP agenda for the government. This includes the development of new policy and legal frameworks as well as the creation of PPP units to strengthen capacities at the national level.

In the four states where specific legislation has been passed or is being drafted, the main issues addressed are project selection, approval and procurement, procedures to deal with unsolicited bids, and the institutional framework. Policies in Kenya and Rwanda highlight the need for project facilitation and Viability Gap Facility (VGF) financing. Frameworks in Tanzania and Kenya pay attention to the need to address fiscal costs and risks and designate responsibilities for these (to the PPP Finance Unit in Tanzania and the PPP Committee in Kenya). Policies in Rwanda and Uganda do not directly address these issues. More detailed descriptions of the frameworks can be found in appendix A, but brief country-level summaries are provided below.

In **Burundi**, there is no explicit PPP framework. All economic and development matters, including PPP issues, are under the second vice president and the Public-Private Dialogue (PPD) Secretariat, which is currently looking into the development of a PPP framework. However, it is not anticipated that the PPD Secretariat will house advisory, monitoring/enforcement, or gatekeeper roles ordinarily associated with PPP Units. The privatization agency (Service Charge des Enterprises Publiques (Burundi) [Service Charge of Public Enterprises; SCEP]) is the technical service for privatizations, which are overseen by a committee of ministries. A privatization law sets the overall framework. A draft bill is under preparation and review.

Kenya's PPP policy was approved by its Cabinet at the beginning of 2012 and a PPP law passed in December 2012. The law provides for a broad definition of PPPs, covering operational contracts through to concessions and land swaps. It could also be interpreted to cover management contracts, but this is not clear. The policy allows unsolicited bids in exceptional circumstances. The PPP Committee is formed of the principal secretaries from relevant departments along with four non-public service experts. It is responsible for overall policy and PPP approvals. The PPP Unit in the Ministry of Finance supports the PPP Committee (figure 1.1).

Kenya has reached financial close on 22 PPPs with over US$4 billion committed investments. Kenya Power and Lighting Company (KPLC) provides the market with reliable energy distribution. With government support, it has been able to increase revenue collections and charge tariffs that allow for cost recovery. This has encouraged the construction of independent power producers (IPPs), which have existed in Kenya since the mid-1990s. The Kenya-Uganda railway is a cross-border PPP, described in appendix C.[3]

Tanzania issued its National PPP Policy in November 2009. A PPP Act was passed in 2010 and the Public Procurement Act was amended in 2011 to

Figure 1.1 Kenya's PPP Institutional Framework

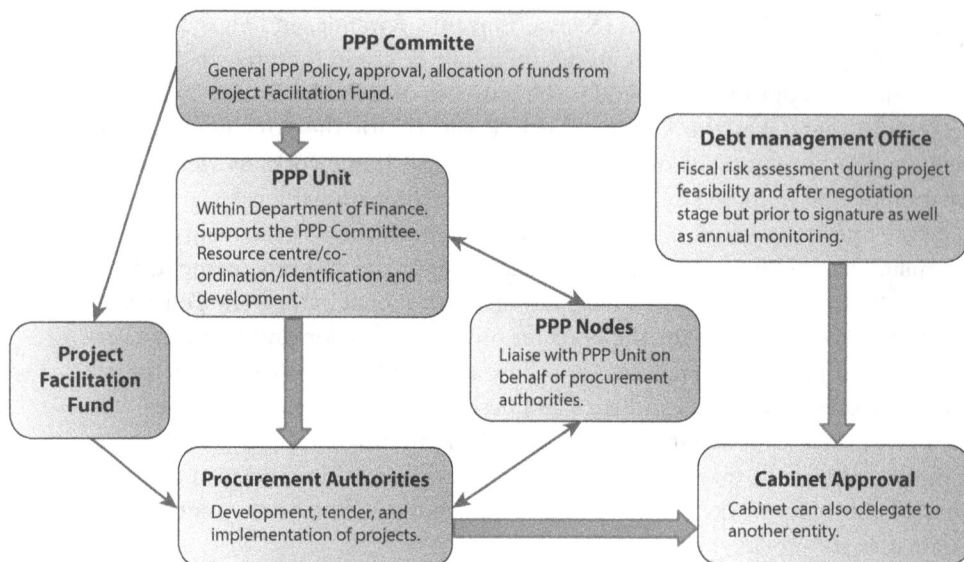

Source: World Bank.
Note: PPP = Public-Private Partnership.

accommodate PPP provisions. The final draft of the PPP regulations is with the Minister of Finance for approval as of mid-2013. Tanzania has also developed a PPP Implementation Strategy and Action Plan and PPP Operational Guidelines. The framework places an emphasis on transparent, competitive procurement. Unsolicited bids are subject to a formal competitive process. The PPP Coordination Unit in the Tanzanian Investment Centre (TIC), which reports to Prime Minister's Office (PMO), and the PPP Finance Unit in the Ministry of Finance were both created by the PPP Act. The former has a promotion role, while the latter examines the fiscal costs of PPPs and the risks being assumed by the government (figure 1.2).

US$3.4 billion has been committed to 21 PPPs in Tanzania. Tanzania Electric Supply Company Limited (TANESCO), the electricity distribution company, has reverted back to state management but there have nevertheless been eight power-related PPPs. The 25-year concession to rehabilitate, operate, and transfer the Kilimanjaro International Airport was cancelled, but the container terminal in Dar es Salaam successfully doubled throughput in the first five years of its operations.

Rwanda's National Public Investment Policy of 2009 makes specific reference to PPPs. A draft PPP law is currently pending submission to parliament. It has a broad definition of PPPs, from management of contracts to concessions and covers a range of sectors. An Inter-Ministerial PPP Steering Committee (IPSC) will provide leadership in development of PPP policies and programs and is responsible for the approval of projects. A PPP Unit, located in the Rwanda Development Board, will assist IPSC and public authorities on all PPP-related

Figure 1.2 Tanzania's PPP Institutional Framework

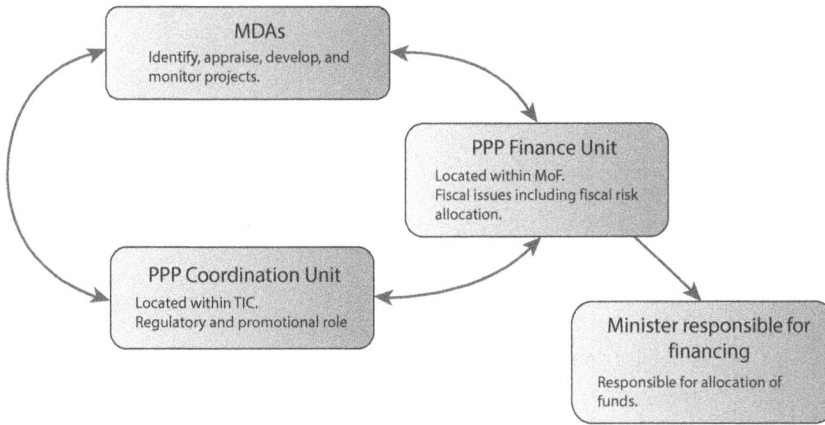

Source: World Bank.
Note: MDA = ministries, departments, and agencies; MoF = Ministry of Finance; PPP = Public-Private Partnership;
TIC = Tanzanian Investment Centre.

matters. Rwanda has PPPs in both the power and telecom sectors. As of mid-2013, IPPs provide the country with only 10 megawatts of electricity.

Uganda's PPP Framework Policy was issued in March 2010 by the Ministry of Finance. The PPP Unit, funded and supervised by the Ministry of Finance, is responsible for supporting and advising government institutions in PPPs. Approval from both the Ministry of Finance and the Cabinet is required after a feasibility study has been carried out. The Ministry of Finance is responsible for the financial implications of any PPP project, but contingent liabilities are not explicitly mentioned. Uganda has the second largest PPP portfolio in the region after Kenya. It has 22 projects that have reached financial close, with investments totaling US$3.5 billion. Aside from telecoms, power is again the largest sector. The Bujagali Hydro Project is much larger than a typical IPP and is projected to provide 250 megawatts of electricity. The Kenya-Uganda railroad is detailed in appendix C.[4]

Partner State Portfolios

This section presents information on private participation in infrastructure in EAC countries using data from the World Bank-Public-Private Infrastructure Advisory Facility (PPIAF) Database (http://ppi.worldbank.org/). It should be noted that the definitions used in this database may not be the same as those used at the country level to define PPPs, but this is the only current comparable data source.

Figure 1.3 shows the total number of projects with private participation in each Partner State as well as the total investment commitments for the period 1990 to 2011. It can be seen that most activity has taken place in the telecoms sector, often in projects with relatively little funding contribution or participation from the public sector. Power has seen the next highest level of activity, with over US$3 billion of investment commitments with private participation in the EAC;

Figure 1.3 Activity in PPPs, by Country and Sector, 1990–2011
US$ million

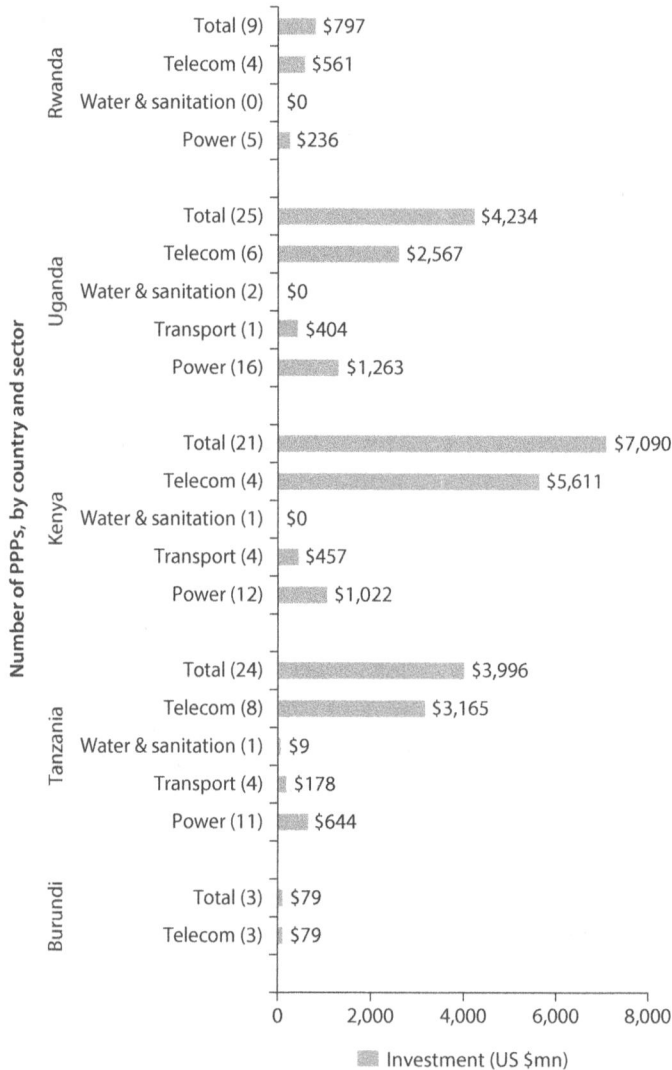

Source: World Bank PPI Database.
Note: PPP = Public-Private Partnership.

transport has seen investment commitments of a little over US$1 billion. At the Partner State level, Kenya has seen the largest volume of investment commitments (over US$7 billion); Uganda has volumes of US$4.2 billion; and Tanzania, US$3.4 billion, although the latter has had the largest number of infrastructure projects with private participation. Burundi has so far only seen activity in the telecoms sector, whereas Rwanda has had five power projects reach financial close.

There has been a relatively consistent level of activity in terms of numbers of projects, although there is some indication of an increase in activity over the last six years, with an average of six projects per year since 2006 (figure 1.4).

Figure 1.4 Number of PPPs in EAC Countries by Year of Financial Close, 1990–2011

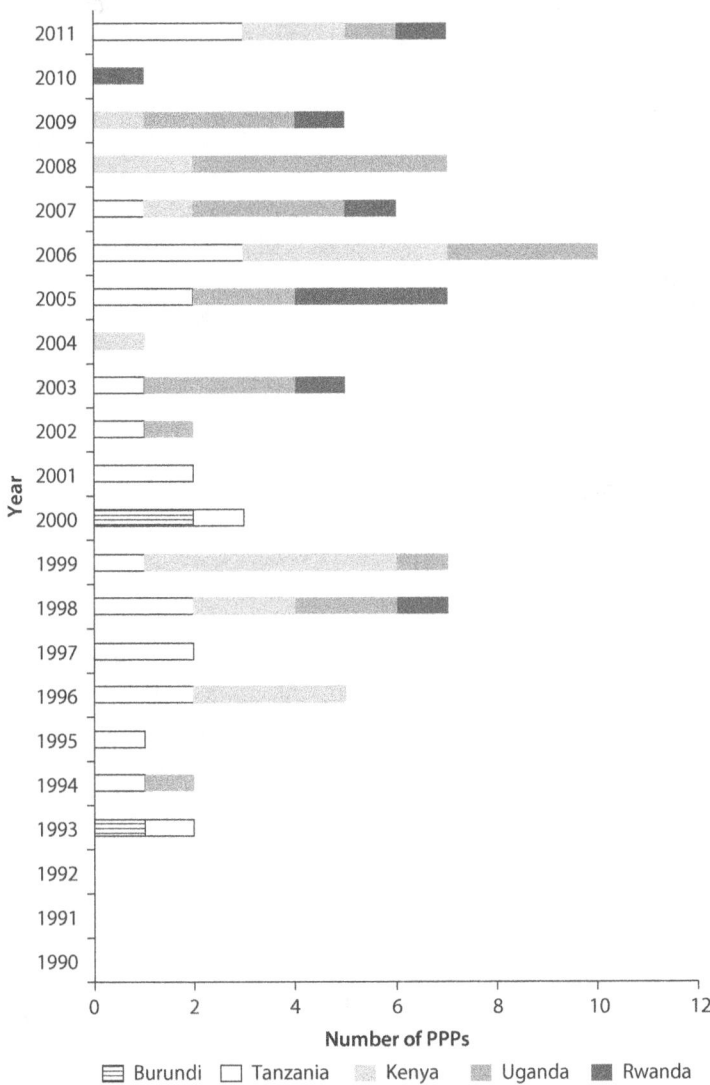

Source: World Bank PPI Database.
Note: PPPs = Public-Private Partnerships.

It is important to note that there have been mixed experiences with these projects. Of the 86 projects in the database, 7 were cancelled or terminated before the end of their envisaged contractual period.

Current Status of Capital Markets

PPPs involve contractual obligations that can extend out for 15–25 years or more. For the private sector to be able to mobilize the financing required to meet the investment needs over this period, there is a tremendous premium on access to equity and long-term debt. While the international capital markets provide a source of foreign currency loans, domestic funds are often harder to obtain with sufficient tenor. This can add considerably to the cost of funds, particularly given uncertainties entailed when continuous refinancing of debt is required to meet PPP obligations. Currently in East Africa, there are very limited longer-term debt sources available. A summary of the evolving capital market development in the subregion's Partner States follows.

Bond markets in East Africa are at a relatively nascent stage, although they have experienced growth in recent years. On the back of an improved macroeconomic environment, governments in the region have taken steps to build their bond markets. The tenors have been extended in all countries; for example, up to 30 years in Kenya, 10 years in Uganda and Tanzania, and 5 years in Rwanda and Burundi. However, the size of the markets is small in all countries, with the exception of Kenya. Kenya had an outstanding domestic debt to gross domestic product (GDP) ratio of 35 percent in 2010, compared to less than 4 percent in Tanzania, Uganda, and Burundi. In Rwanda, the ratio was only 0.3 percent. The relatively deeper bond market in Kenya is attributed to the fact that Kenya extensively uses the bond market to finance its fiscal deficit.

There is very limited liquidity in the secondary bond markets, except in Uganda and Kenya. There is significant work required to build benchmark bonds to develop more credible yield curves that would be useful as pricing references for nongovernment issues. The yield curves in Kenya, Uganda, and Tanzania have generally shifted down since the introduction of longer-dated securities (see figure 1.5). There has also been increased convergence in the longer-term rates in three of the five Partner States. The recent interest rate volatility experienced in Kenya is not conducive to bond issuance and has led to a delay in the issuance of new corporate bonds. Monetary authorities in the

Figure 1.5 East African Yield Curves, December 31, 2011

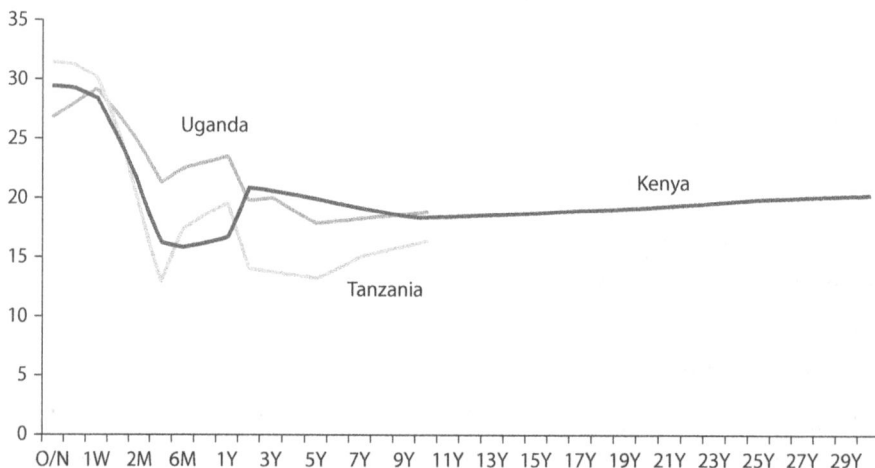

Source: Standard Chartered Bank.

region need to be able to implement effective policies to stabilize the markets if their ability to raise long-term funds for infrastructure and other priority sectors is to be maintained and augmented.

The nongovernment bond markets in East Africa are at an even more nascent stage, accounting for only 1.7 percent of the combined GDP in the region. Despite the low level of issuance, there is great diversity in the issuers. Sectors including utilities (infrastructure), telecoms, banking, microfinance, and agriculture have all issued bonds, signifying the potential of the corporate bond markets. There has been strong growth, albeit from a low base, in the markets over the last five years. The largest so far was a US$350 million infrastructure issue by Kenya Electricity Generating Company, demonstrating that a well-structured issue can raise significant amounts in the market (see figure 1.6). The market is largely dominated by Kenya, although the volume is growing in both Tanzania and Uganda. Obstacles to increased corporate bond issuance in East Africa include competition from a liquid banking sector, a cumbersome and "merit-based" approval process geared to equities, and the limited number of good quality issuers and well-packaged projects.

There have been reforms over the past four years in the nongovernment bond markets, aimed at improving the primary market issuance framework, deepening the secondary markets, building capacity, regionalizing markets, and supporting demonstration transactions. Reforms have also been aimed at lowering the costs and improving the speed of accessing the bond markets while providing a framework for new financing structures, such as asset-backed securities. The latter are

Figure 1.6 Cumulative Corporate Bond Issues in East Africa

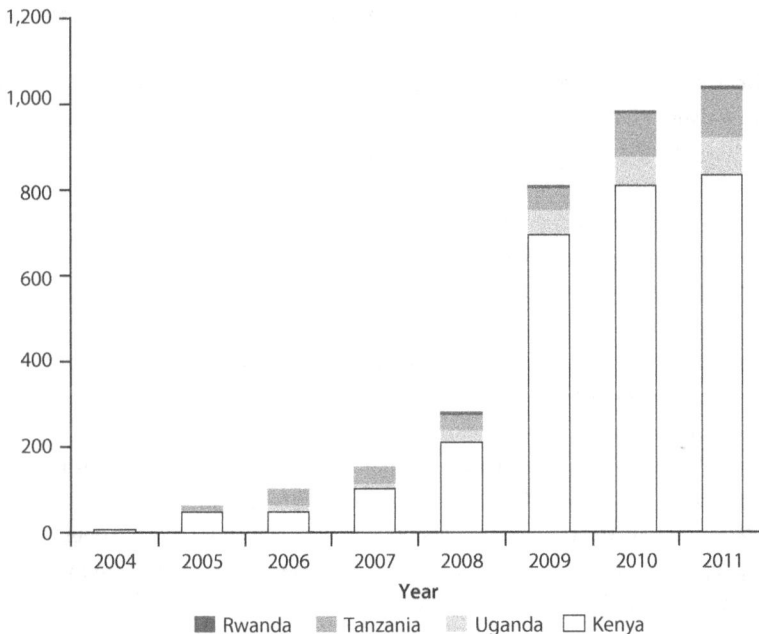

Legend: Rwanda, Tanzania, Uganda, Kenya

Source: Efficient Securities Markets Institutional Development.

Building Integrated Markets within the East African Community
http://dx.doi.org/10.1596/978-1-4648-0227-0

particularly important by enabling the use of securitization techniques for infra-structure financing and the use of Special Purpose Vehicles to raise funds. Regulators are currently implementing a more flexible framework for the issu-ance of regional bonds that would be better suited for issuers such as the East African Development Bank (EADB). The requirements for regional bond issu-ance are described in box 1.1.

The absence of longer-term financing and the relatively embryonic state of bond markets pose significant challenges to the sourcing of funds for infrastruc-ture PPPs. These challenges are exacerbated by the limited project finance expertise of commercial banks in the region. While there are exceptions, com-mercial banks tend to favor other investment opportunities where they can bet-ter match the deposit capital with shorter lending tenures. Should the EAC choose to further develop its regional infrastructure, the gap that currently exists in the debt market could present a significant constraint to PPP investment. However, it is first necessary to develop a commercially attractive pipeline of projects. This would provide the market drivers for further development of lon-ger-term debt financing instruments.

Box 1.1 Requirements for Regional Bond Issuance

The East African Member States Securities Regulatory Authorities (EASRA) has approved a framework for regional bond issuance under a single prospectus. The framework being ad-opted in Partner States has already been exposed to public comment in Kenya and Uganda. Although the frameworks for the issuance of bonds in Partner States are highly harmonized, there has been no overarching framework/process to facilitate regional issues. Salient fea-tures of the proposed framework include:

- **Shelf facility**: Up to three years. This provides significant flexibility to issuers who can reg-ister a new issue in each of the four countries' markets for a period of up to three years—aligning borrowing to funding requirements for the projects.
- **Disclosure framework**: New framework is largely "disclosure based," allowing entities without a track record to issue bonds.
- **Ratio analysis and credit enhancement**: Debt ratios such as total debt/net worth and funds from operations/total debt have been dropped, while mandatory credit enhance-ment is no longer required.
- **Professional parties**: This includes accountants, legal advisors, arrangers, and sponsoring brokers. They do not have to be licensed or registered in each Partner State. This will sig-nificantly cut professional fees for regional issues.
- **Fees**: Regulators to share a combined evaluation fee of 0.1 percent, with a maximum cap. This is a potential cost saving of up to 0.4 percent in approval fees.
- **Credit ratings**: Mandatory for regional issues. However, the rating agency does not have to be registered in the region provided it meets the International Organization of Securi-ties Commissions (IOSCO) code of conduct for rating agencies.

Existing Capacities and Activities of EAC

The objectives of the EAC are "to develop policies and programs aimed at widening and deepening co-operation among the Partner States in political, economic, social and cultural fields, research and technology, defense, security and legal and judicial affairs, for their mutual benefit," and the EAC Treaty sets out a number of operational principles, including "the provision by the Partner States of an adequate and appropriate enabling environment, such as conducive policies and basic infrastructure." As the EAC moves forward in developing its support for PPP frameworks in the region, it will also need to address how this support is delivered.

A number of organizations and institutions within the EAC work to develop the enabling environment for infrastructure provision, which can also help to address the specific requirements needed to foster regional PPP approaches. For example:

- The EAC Secretariat has a Deputy Secretary General (DSG) devoted to Planning and Infrastructure (which includes Transport, Civil Aviation, Communications and Investment, and Private Sector Development) and another DSG devoted to Productive and Social Sectors (which includes Energy, Environment and Natural Resources, Education, and Health).
- The EAC Assembly has committees that correspond to the departments of the Secretariat.
- The EAC Council has Sectoral Committees focused on key infrastructure issues such as transport.

These bodies have developed policies and legislation related to the development and management of infrastructure in the region. For example, the legislative assembly has passed a number of acts focused on harmonization and promotion of infrastructure and natural resource developments, such as the Lake Victoria Transport Management Act 2007, the EAC Civil Aviation Safety and Security Oversight Agency Act 2009, and the Standards, Measurement, Quantities and Testing Act 2006 (as amended in 2010). The EAC is currently considering legislation for one-stop border posts and harmonization of axle loads for vehicles. The Secretariat has played and continues to play a key role in coordination and development of these initiatives.

A number of regional institutions are independent of but have connections to the EAC through memoranda of understanding (MoUs) or other links, and may play a key role in the regional PPP agenda. These include the Central Corridor Transit Transport Facilitation Agency (CCTTFA) and the Northern Corridor Coordination Authority (NCCA). These regional institutions are established by agreement between states that may include some or all of the Partner States of the EAC and other relevant states (for example, CCTTFA was formed between Burundi, the Democratic Republic of Congo [DRC], Rwanda, Tanzania, and Uganda; NCCA operates between Kenya, Rwanda, Uganda, Burundi, and the

DRC). The MoUs seek to promote the development of transport infrastructure, transit transport, customs, and trade facilitation with a view to enhancing development in the subregions covered by those corridors.

Two autonomous institutions of particular note for the regional PPP agenda are the Lake Victoria Basin Commission (LVBC) and the EADB, described in more detail below.

The Lake Victoria Basin Commission: The LVBC was established pursuant to the Protocol for Sustainable Development of the Lake Victoria Basin of November 2003 by the Council of Ministers of the EAC "for the sustainable development and management of the Lake Victoria Basin." Its responsibilities include development of infrastructure and services around the lake, promotion of trade, commerce, and infrastructure, and sustainable development, management, and equitable utilization of water resources. The LVBC plays a key role in improving the enabling environment for lake users and private operators on the lake. The Lake Victoria Transport Management Act establishes, among other things, lake safety standards. The LVBC is also currently involved in a significant initiative focused on environmental sustainability. Another recent LVBC initiative organized an investor forum for promotion of investment on and around the lake, in coordination with the EAC Secretariat. The LVBC could play a potential role in selection, preparation, and promotion of PPP projects and coordination with Partner States on procurement of PPP projects around the lake.

The East African Development Bank: As the key regional EAC financial institution, the EADB is another autonomous institution that can help take the PPP agenda forward. It is 86.3 percent owned by its four country members, with Kenya, Tanzania, and Uganda holding equal shares of 26.4 percent. Rwanda in the process of building to a similar level, and Burundi is in the process of applying for membership. The African Development Bank (AfDB), the German Development Finance Corporation (DEG), and the Netherlands Development Finance Company (FMO) hold a combined 12.8 percent share (Class B shares) and an additional 0.9 percent is owned by six private banking entities. In addition to government representatives and an AfDB representative, there are four private directors on the board who are prominent businessmen and -women in their respective countries.

The EADB has operated continuously, reasonably successfully, with a regional mandate since its establishment in 1967. Since 1995, it has approved a total of 549 loans valued at US$763 million. Based on data available as of October 2011, the EADB has US$248 million in total assets, US$144 million in net worth (41 percent of total assets), and 110 projects in a loan portfolio valued at US$83 million, of which 14.0 percent (24 projects) are presently nonperforming. Its future prospects for raising additional equity when needed are robust as it has US$443 million in additional callable capital from its member countries. While the EADB has recently focused on corporate lending to medium- and smaller-sized companies, it does have some experience with both regional and infrastructure projects, on which it has now been directed by its board to focus more attention. It has already lent US$49.8 million to seven projects within these two categories in recent years. Five of these projects have been fully implemented and all are operating successfully.

The EADB has been managed conservatively during the past three years, focusing effectively on cleaning up its portfolio, collecting bad debts, strengthening human resources, and building a strong foundation for future expansion and effective performance of a key role it hopes to play in supporting future EAC and East African Community Development Fund (EACDF) activities in support of regional and infrastructure finance. The EADB currently has a Fitch credit rating of B- (with a stable outlook), but rating improvements are anticipated over the coming periods now that the Tanzanian court has dismissed a legal case brought against it. A summary of its operational and financial performance and factors bearing on its overall governance is provided in appendix F (based on an assessment undertaken in 2011). Notwithstanding the relatively strong standing of the EADB, its image in the marketplace and among relevant donors is mixed for a variety of reasons, including (i) the need for large write-offs of bad loans prior to 2009; (ii) a generally poor reputation shared by most of Africa's Development Finance Institutions (DFIs); (iii) the 86 percent combined government ownership position, which worries some donors; and (iv) its small size relative to relevant private commercial institutions in the region.

The EADB has had a pioneering role in the history and development of bond markets in East Africa. It had a debut issue in Kenya in 1996 and has subsequently issued in Uganda and Tanzania with repeat issues in all three markets. The EADB bond was the first instrument listed on the Uganda Securities Exchange while the Kenyan issue preceded floating rate Treasury bond issues. In 2010, three bond issues in Kenya, Uganda, and Tanzania were outstanding in its books, with a face value of US$8.6 million. The Kenyan issue, which had a tenure of seven years, matured in August 2011, while the Tanzanian and Ugandan issues were set to mature in 2012. The EADB has had an excellent track record with its bond issues without registering any default. Despite this long history of tapping the local bond markets, the issuances appear to be relatively opportunistic and the size of issues relatively small. The last issue was in December 2005.

Notes

1. Note that data for Burundi were not available at the time of the AICD research.
2. An entrepôt is a trading post where merchandise can be imported and exported without paying import duties, often at a profit.
3. Interview with Eng. Stanley Kamau, Director of PPP Unit, Kenya.
4. Interview with David Ssebabi and Otweyo Orono, Privatisation Unit, Uganda.

Building Integrated Markets within the East African Community
http://dx.doi.org/10.1596/978-1-4648-0227-0

CHAPTER 2

Lessons Learned from Regional Project Case Studies

Summary of Country Case Studies

Detailed studies of three regional Public-Private Partnership (PPP) projects were conducted and can be found in appendixes C, D, and E. Chosen to best illustrate some of the challenges involved in cross-border transactions, the three case studies are: (i) the Rift Valley Railway (RVR); (ii) the Mozambique to South Africa Toll Road (MSATR); and (iii) the West African Gas Pipeline (WAGP). These projects were selected because of the following:

- Being based in Sub-Saharan Africa, they were seen as most relevant to the East Africa region.
- They cover the power and transport sectors, areas with the most potential for PPPs in the East African Community (EAC).
- They include a variety of institutional structures, both bilateral (RVR, MSATR) and multicountry (WAGP).
- They use a variety of innovative treaty and contractual arrangements to solve cross-border difficulties, illustrating both the limits and potential of Regional Economic Community (REC) involvement (for example, Southern African Development Community [SADC], Economic Community of West African States [ECOWAS]).

This report contains a summary of case studies with a discussion on some of the key lessons learned, particularly as they relate to the potential role of RECs.

Rift Valley Railway

The RVR covers 2,350 kilometers, connecting the port of Mombasa to Nairobi and Kisumu in Kenya and to Kampala and the oil fields at Lake Albert on Uganda's border with the Democratic Republic of Congo (DRC). Recently, it has been carrying loads far below its potential; in 2010, it carried only 1.6 million tons. One of the key features of the concession awarded in 2006 was to upgrade the infrastructure to reach 5 million tons per annum by 2011.

As a cross-border PPP, new contractual arrangements were required, including the creation of two separate concession companies under one holding company that would be linked by an "interface agreement." Each of the two companies was awarded a 25-year concession. This came with a commitment to provide passenger services for at least five years and to upgrade the infrastructure. The winning bid entailed a concession fee of 11.1 percent of gross revenue plus upfront fees. This was higher than expected and more than that of equivalent projects. A Joint Railway Commission was set up as an advisory body to resolve cross-border issues relating to the concession.

By 2010, the deal was on the verge of collapse. Freight volumes were 7–10 percent below target; investments reached only US$1.2 million of the planned US$7 million, and passenger services were 32 percent below commitment. In January 2009, the International Finance Corporation (IFC) and Kreditanstalt für Wiederaufbau (Reconstruction Credit Institute; KfW), both lenders to the deal, signaled to commence the cure period,[1] allowing the major lender to step in. An agreement was reached on a new financing plan, endorsed by all parties. The new financing plan increased investment from US$111 million to US$311 million. Presently much of the investment is being carried out, although traffic volumes have yet to pick up. It remains to be seen whether the railroad will become profitable again.

The deal reveals some of the difficulties involved in cross-border infrastructure. As there was no standard legal and regulatory script to follow, much of it had to be innovated. This includes the aforementioned "interface agreement" that provided for the establishment of an advisory Joint Railway Commission. Deeper regulatory integration would have potentially helped remove some of the barriers to integration in a more effective way that the interface agreement is able do.

Mozambique to South Africa Toll Road
The Mozambique to South Africa Toll Road (N4) was a pioneering PPP. It was the first toll road in Sub-Saharan Africa and the second regional PPP of any kind. It was part of a much larger plan for the development of the Maputo corridor and, having been signed in 1997, has had 15 years of successful implementation. However, it has not proven to be the model for other PPPs as expected, and in some ways its success can be explained by a few unique features.

The road had high-level political backing. Most of the road was also already built and carrying the minimum amount of traffic required to support a commercial operation, with a long history of transport on the corridor. Although it is a cross-border road, 423 kilometers out of 503 kilometers are located inside South Africa. Partly due to the high level of political interest in the project, it was carried out in a fast-track, top-down fashion. The process was very much driven by South Africa's Department of Transport, which had experience and technical expertise. The speed with which the transaction was driven resulted in bids being requested before Mozambique even had a legal framework in place for toll roads.

This regional project was one of 180 commercial projects identified as part of the Maputo Development Corridor. The fast-track approach led by the South African Department of Transport meant there was little room for consultation, even with Mozambique. The Southern African Development Community (SADC) had no real role to play.

West African Gas Pipeline

The West African Gas Pipeline transports gas from Nigeria to Benin, Togo, and Ghana. It consists of 680 kilometers of onshore and offshore pipeline and cost US$900 million to build, 52 percent more than estimated. The project was conceived by the Economic Community of West African States (ECOWAS) as a tool for regional integration and a supply of natural gas into the West African Power Pool (WAPP). Although the development of the pipeline was first proposed in 1982, the Inter-Governmental Agreement was only signed in 2000. The pipeline began commercial operation in 2011. The pipeline is owned and operated by the West African Gas Pipeline Company (WAGPCo), a special purpose vehicle. Chevron is the largest shareholder in WAGPCo, while the Nigerian National Petroleum Company, among others, also has a stake. The International Development Association (IDA) provided a US$50 million Partial Risk Guarantee (PRG) and the Multilateral Investment Guarantee Agency (MIGA), a US$75 million political risk insurance.

The project managed to overcome the problems of regional governance and has been a success. Three main mechanisms were used to achieve regime standardization: (i) the West African Gas Pipeline Treaty; (ii) the International Project Agreement; and (iii) individual state enabling legislation. The WAGP Treaty established the WAGP Authority as a regulatory authority for WAGPCo. The International Project Agreement established a harmonized investment regime to allow WAGPCo to operate as a single business across the four countries. It also established the tariff methodology principles and a dispute mechanism. Enabling legislation was passed in all four countries to allow WAGP activity to take place as though in a single fiscal regime. This included a uniform income tax rate and accounting treatment.

The significance attached to this project by the four countries involved can be seen by the speed with which their enabling legislations were enacted. This was a major factor in the project's success. The project is commercially viable and estimated to provide the four states with US$634 million in tax revenue over the project's life. The broad integration agenda of ECOWAS is reflected in the exemplary cooperation between the four contracting states.

Key Questions and Lessons in Defining a Role for RECs

The three case study projects are distinctively different. However, they suggest that while "bilateral" regional PPP projects such as the RVR and the MSATR are more efficiently done between the stakeholder states, those involving more than two countries—such as the WAGP—derive additional benefits from the more active involvement of a REC, notably in facilitating a multinational treaty and multicountry harmonization. When it comes to lessons learned from these case studies regarding the role that a REC can constructively play, a number of questions need to be considered, such as those outlined below.

Are there ways in which RECs could add value to regional PPPs, especially with upstream legal-regulatory harmonization? The success of the WAGP shows the importance that upstream supportive policy leadership can play. In the case of the WAGP, the comparative advantage that ECOWAS had in formulating and promoting a regional policy was important in providing the platform for this initiative and attracting international finance. Another important area of contribution can be the facilitation of project-specific harmonization, as evidenced by the creation of a single fiscal regime for this program. In contrast, the RVR case lacked a wider regional policy context and, rather than harmonization, relied on an interface agreement to provide a vehicle to address difficulties in a more "ad hoc" manner. The other alternative is, in many ways, represented by the case of the N4 toll road. There was neither regional policy nor harmonization; rather, a "dominant" country took the lead. However, this last case reflected some unique differences in capacity that existed at that time between South Africa and Mozambique. This is not the situation among the Partner States of the EAC. This suggests the need for greater upstream policy, legal, and regulatory harmonization, at least initially, on a project by project basis.

Do RECs have the skills needed for this—or can they "buy" the skills of consultants? In all three cases, the role of the respective REC was limited. To some extent, this reflects their lack of technical expertise and capacity. Critical policy and political expertise resided within ECOWAS and was clearly deployed in the case of the WAGP. But more downstream PPP sector and project technical expertise is absent in all the RECs. The South Africa Department of Transport had far more experience than SADC in road building and this allowed them to take a lead without much collaboration. In the case of the RVR, PPP expertise resided in the Kenya and Uganda Ministries of Finance, albeit expertise that to a large extent was acquired "on the job" as the two ministries sought to resolve contract issues. RECs need to be selective in the development and provision of technical expertise which, in most cases, is best deployed at a country level.

Does REC involvement in a cross-border PPP complicate or slow implementation? Furthermore, what degree of slow-down is worth stronger regional consultation, participation, and preparation? In the case of the WAGP, REC involvement did arguably slow the pace early in the process, but this served to ensure that a sounder WAGP project was eventually brought into existence, as key issues such as fiscal regime harmonization were resolved, which in turn increased the chances of success. The WAGP case shows that where there is political will, the resistance to passing enabling legislation may not be too great. The RVR case demonstrates the difficulties of resolving problems that are later encountered without well-established mechanisms. While the N4 toll road was fast-tracked, such an approach would normally have led to sustainability problems for the PPP. The fact that it is the only such project in existence 15 years after closure shows its dependence on its unique success factors.

Do RECs have a role in providing preparation funding for regional projects? Preparation costs for regional projects are much higher than for domestic projects, amounting to some 8–10 percent of project investment (Leigland 2010a). The RVR project would likely have been more successful with more investment in project preparation. In addition, if RECs were able to provide funds for the preparation stage of regional projects, they would have leverage to become more relevant and further influence the development of the regional PPP agenda.

Can RECs play a supporting role in regional projects without expecting to direct or "own" them? ECOWAS played a key supporting role in the WAGP case. As well as proposing the project as far back as 1982, its broad agenda of regional integration and its position as a unifying body helped to ensure cooperation between the four countries. It is important for national governments to "own" and drive projects located within their boundaries. It can be harder to establish relationships of trust between RECs and their members unless it is clear that the members are the ultimate decision makers. Where RECs act as diplomats, facilitators, interlocutors, interpreters, advisors, and so on, they can carve out meaningful roles on regional PPPs.

Note

1. A "cure period" is a specific provision in a contract allowing a defaulting party to correct the cause of default.

Building Integrated Markets within the East African Community
http://dx.doi.org/10.1596/978-1-4648-0227-0

CHAPTER 3

Regional PPP Policy Framework Issues

Key Considerations for a Regional PPP Policy

Given the current enabling environment for Public-Private Partnerships (PPPs) and the current scope and capacity of the East African Community (EAC) in this arena, there will be substantial challenges to be met to scale up the use of PPPs to meet basic service needs in the EAC. The most important of these are as follows:

- **Fragmentation and small market size:** All Partner States are, on a global scale, small markets for PPPs. The projects will typically be smaller than those on offer in many Asian, North American, European, and Latin American markets. There will also be relatively fewer repeat projects on offer than in larger markets. All of these make the upfront costs of entry into a market, and engaging in a specific project, relatively high compared to project values and can dissuade foreign investors from entering these markets. Presenting the Partner States as a genuinely single market will reduce barriers to entry, but this will in turn require efforts to converge PPP approaches and instruments so that this is credible.
- **Low capacity:** PPPs are new in the region, and thus require legal and commercial skills not often present in government. Establishing these skills will be a challenge, and given the frequent turnover of staff, a greater challenge still will be maintaining them over time. This can mean that skills built up in one transaction are lost thereafter if individuals transfer to other posts. Partner States will find it a challenge to maintain a critical mass of capacity and institutional knowledge in government agencies working on PPPs. It may also be the case that the capacities used to develop a new transaction in the EAC could be deployed in another Partner State, yet there are few opportunities for doing this at present.
- **Misplaced stakeholder expectations:** There have been negative experiences with PPPs for both public and private sector stakeholders in the EAC Partner States. As noted above, PPPs can fail for a number of reasons. One frequently occurring factor is a lack of realism on the part of both government

and the private sector. Governments are often disappointed because they expect the private sector to bring a larger volume of financing, which the latter might not do because it is not supported by project cash flows. The private sector may have unrealistic expectations about the government's ability to improve the policy and regulatory framework. Regardless of the precise causes, a range of stakeholders have negative perceptions of PPPs and their possible benefits.

• **Inability to coordinate on and structure regional PPPs:** Some projects that are regional in nature might best be executed as PPPs. Under current approaches, there is no coordinating framework for bringing together countries to contract or manage projects jointly, possibly increasing the costs to the private sector of engaging with the Partner States, nor are there clear mechanisms for sharing project costs among the beneficiaries.

• **Regional project financing gaps:** Regional aspects of infrastructure projects can often entail additional costs—both in terms of preparation and project investment costs. While these costs are often fully justified in terms of the regional benefits they generate, these benefits are often not captured by the party/country incurring the cost. For instance, developing internal container ports for shipments to landlocked EAC countries would not necessarily be a first priority for Kenya or Tanzania, given other more immediate national investment needs. Similarly, cross-border infrastructure linkages may not justify the investment cost based on a country-specific cost-benefit analysis. Regionally sourced funding could serve to correct for this type of market failure.

This suggests a role for the EAC in addressing these market and institutional failures in a fashion that complements the ongoing actions of the Partner States. At the Regional Workshop on "Public-Private Partnerships as Viable Options for EAC Regional Integration/Infrastructural Development," held in Nairobi on August 25–26, 2011, and the subsequent Experts' Workshop held in Arusha from October 24–26, 2011, stakeholders were asked to consider the constraints that PPPs faced in the EAC and the activities the EAC could undertake to address these. The discussion highlighted the role that EAC could play in (i) increasing awareness of PPPs among different stakeholders including the private sector; (ii) improving technical capacity to develop PPP projects and frameworks; (iii) financing regional infrastructure PPP investments; (iv) developing a database and other mechanisms for sharing information on progress on PPPs; and (v) conducting training for a range of stakeholders.

There was a perception among stakeholders that the EAC could significantly add to what is being done at the national level. The activities outlined and discussed by stakeholders focused on the EAC's role as a convener, but also suggested it might consider investing in additional resources to provide capacities and funding to engage in PPPs. It was also noted that to do this and to add value to Partner States' ongoing activities, it would have to bring in capacities and knowledge on PPPs at least equal to that present at the national level. Additional areas of potential EAC engagement, as discussed at these stakeholder events, included convening and coordinating, promoting PPPs with investors, harmonizing, developing guidance on key issues including fiscal risks, and facilitating regional projects via the coordination of procurement and development of standardized provisions. The country consultations undertaken during May 2012 also showed broad support for the EAC playing a convening and capacity building role, financing PPPs, and facilitating regional approaches. It was noted that efforts by the EAC should complement, not overlap with or substitute for, what national governments are doing in this space.

A framework to address this to be developed by the EAC could comprise the following areas: (i) a policy for PPPs at the EAC level; (ii) a focal point and center of expertise for PPPs in the community; and (iii) funding and financing options for regional PPPs. The next section examines each of these areas in turn.

EAC Regional PPP Policy: Key Areas of Priority and Options

There is currently no EAC policy or framework on PPPs although, as noted in chapter 2, there are a number of EAC initiatives and institutions focused on infrastructure which are likely to result in an improved regional enabling environment for PPPs. Any policy developed at the EAC level would have to complement what is happening at the Partner State level. This section sets out the main issues that an EAC regional policy on PPPs would have to address as well as some of the choices that could be made.

There was consensus at the Experts' Workshop in Arusha to develop a policy framework for regional PPPs that could serve as a signal to potential investors of the importance the EAC places on PPPs and as a guide to how the EAC and Partner States are working together to support and enable regional PPPs. Provision of basic infrastructure is one of the operational principles of the EAC.[1] Key aspects of this include harmonization of regulatory laws, rules, and practices, construction and maintenance of infrastructure in Partner States, and review and redesign of intermodal transport systems.[2] The EAC Council has the power to make policy statements on particular issues, which can be a first step towards developing legislation or issuing other binding instruments. The Experts' Workshop recommended that the policy should:

- Give some background on the EAC and initiatives that will foster the enabling environment for PPP development, such as the axle load and one-stop border post initiatives and the work of the Lake Victoria Basin Commission.
- Describe the significant steps that each Partner State has taken to strengthen its own enabling environment to facilitate and promote PPPs within its own jurisdiction.
- Develop a definition for regional PPP projects.
- Formalize areas where the EAC can play a role in facilitating regional PPP projects.

Based on the findings and discussions with stakeholders at the regional work-shops and country consultations, the objectives of a regional policy could include the following, without a presumption that all would be acted on immediately:

- Develop a clear framework for selecting and developing regional PPPs to pro-vide certainty to investors and establish incentives for projects with a regional dimension to stimulate investment in public infrastructure and related ser-vices in the EAC region.
- Create a mechanism for the sharing of knowledge and experience on program development and lessons learnt from each Partner State's PPP program to ensure that future PPP projects are sustainable and successful.
- Market the EAC as a common investment destination for infrastructure, building on economies of scale to develop and promote projects; combined, the size of the potential PPP portfolio for the region is significantly larger than that of each Partner State and could be more attractive to potential investors.
- Develop expertise at the regional level that can provide technical assistance to Partner States that might be difficult to obtain at a state level.
- Find regional solutions to the lack of long-term financing to support project preparation and to fund viability gaps in regional projects, and coordinate with the donor community.

A key issue is whether an EAC PPP policy should seek to just address issues around regional PPPs alone or to harmonize the framework for all PPPs in the EAC, be they national (or subnational) projects or regional ones. At the present time, while national PPP frameworks are being developed and are evolving, it is recommended that any policy seek to complement what is being developed at the national level by focusing on regional projects. Over time, convergence and harmonization of approaches in PPPs in the Partner States might facilitate the implementation of a single-policy framework for all PPPs in the EAC. But this should be a longer-term consideration based on lessons learned from developing and implementing a first round of national and regional PPP projects under the newly evolving PPP frameworks. It will also be necessary to agree on the appli-cable definition of PPPs, what constitutes a "regional" PPP, the scope of applica-tion (for example, which sectors?) and principles and guidelines for project selection, preparation, and modalities of Partner State cooperation. These issues are considered below.

Definitions of PPPs: There is no one generally accepted definition of a PPP in international practice. Broadly speaking, a PPP is a long-term contract between a private party and a government agency for providing a public asset or service in which the private party bears significant risk and management responsibility. Some examples currently in use are provided in box 3.1. In practice, there are many different arrangements, ranging from PPPs providing new assets and ser-vices to those covering existing assets and services. Definitions need to cover PPPs in which the private party is paid entirely by service users and those in which a government agency makes some or all of the payments.

Box 3.1 Examples of PPP Definitions Used Around the World

The **European Union** does not have a single definition of PPPs, but one of its guidance notes refers to PPPs as "the transfer to the private sector of investment projects that traditionally have been executed or financed by the public sector."

In **Brazil**, the PPP Law states that PPP contracts are agreements entered into between the government or public entities and private entities that establish a legally binding obligation to manage (in whole or in part) services, undertakings, and activities in the public interest where the private sector is responsible for financing investment and management. (It should be noted that Brazil has separate laws for concessions and PPPs.)

In **India**, a PPP is defined as a partnership between a public sector entity and a private sector entity (must have 51 percent or more of the equity with the private partner) for the creation and/or management of infrastructure for public purpose for a specified period of time. It must be on commercial terms, with the private partner procured through a transparent and open procurement system.

The Partner States have adopted different approaches to defining PPPs. In Uganda, the policy defines a PPP as a medium- to long-term contractual arrangement between public and private sectors to finance, construct/renovate, manage, and/or maintain a public infrastructure, or the provision of a public service that involves the sharing of risks and rewards and delivers desired policy outcomes that are in the public interest. The Tanzania PPP Act 2010 defines them as "projects undertaken in partnership between the public and private sectors." In Kenya, a PPP is an agreement between a public entity and a private party under which (i) the private party undertakes to perform a public function or provide a service on behalf of the public entity; and (ii) the private party receives a benefit for performing the function, either by way of compensation from a public fund, charges, or fees collected by a private party from users or customers of a service provided to them or combination of such compensation and charges or fees; the private party is generally liable for risks arising from the performance depending on the terms of the agreement. It is recommended that for the regional policy, a definition of PPPs be developed that draws on the Partner States' definitions and establishes a common standard acceptable to all.

Definition of a regional project: The Experts' Workshop recommended developing a definition of regional PPPs to determine the scope of the policy and those projects where EAC support may be appropriate. There was extensive discussion as to what should constitute a regional PPP at the two workshops and it was recommended that the definition should include projects that include a cross-border aspect, such as a road or transmission line, and projects that, while situated in one Partner State, play a significant role in infrastructure service provision and economic growth for one or more other Partner States. This definition is also consistent with the Treaty which requires, for instance, coastal Partner States to cooperate with the landlocked Partner States and grant them easy access, for instance, to port facilities and opportunities to participate in provision of port and maritime services. In providing this definition, it is noted that Partner States would be free to develop projects wholly within their territories as national projects, even if they were regional projects as defined above.

Scope of a regional PPP policy: Based on the above, the policy would provide a definition of PPPs and apply it to the selection and development of regional PPPs, and would create a framework for sharing knowledge between Partner States. The sectors covered by the policy would, at least initially, focus on traditional infrastructure sectors such as power, transport, water, and information and communication technology (ICT). As the regional PPP program developed, consideration could be given to potential for developing regional social services, such as schools and hospitals.

Principles for selection, preparation, and procurement of regional PPPs: A regional PPP policy would need to set out the main principles by which regional projects would be selected, procured, and prepared. It would make sense to draw on principles in the PPP policies of the Partner States. These could include value for money (VfM), affordability, transparency and accountability, output orientation, and public interest (cost-benefit assessment). An objective mechanism for prioritizing projects on this basis would have to be developed and addressed.

Fostering Partner State cooperation in regional PPP development: The key areas of cooperation proposed are (i) knowledge exchange and capacity building; (ii) selection, preparation, procurement, and prioritization of regional projects; (iii) standard setting and harmonization; and (iv) financing PPPs.

EAC Regional PPP Resource Center: Issues and Options

Creating a focal point for PPPs: The role that a regional PPP resource center can play in strengthening national level PPP capacities within a REC has already been recognized. Box 3.2 presents three examples of efforts at the regional level to develop centralized PPP resources designed to strengthen and supplement national resources.

Box 3.2 International Experience with PPP Focal Points within Regional Economic Communities

The European PPP Expertise Center (EPEC) is a joint initiative of the European Investment Bank (EIB), the European Commission, and European Union Member States and Candidate Countries and is the foremost example of a regional PPP initiative. Created in 2008 and physically housed in the EIB headquarters in Luxembourg, its staffing complement includes EIB

---

box continues next page

Box 3.2 International Experience with PPP Focal Points within Regional Economic Communities (continued)

staff seconded to the EPEC as well as secondments from Member States' PPP units. The EPEC's mandate is to strengthen the capacity of its public sector members to enter into PPP transactions through a program of activities that include the following:

- Collaborative work—EPEC members work together on particular issues of common interest; recently, this has included papers on state guarantees for PPPs and procurement of PPPs.
- Institutional strengthening—the EPEC will field teams to work with individual members on specific aspects of their PPP programs, providing a "peer review" process.
- A helpdesk gives rapid responses to immediate questions, or redirects questions to other members with relevant expertise.

It is important to emphasize that the EPEC does not play the role of a regional PPP Unit analogous to a national unit—it does not clear or approve projects, for example, nor does it provide advisory services on project structuring. As outlined above, its activities focus mainly on capacity building support. The EPEC has not played an active role in the coordination of cross-border or regional PPP projects in the European Union (EU) to date, although it may increase its activities in these areas in the future. It organizes consultative forums with the private sector twice a year. The EPEC also supports countries outside of the EU (including accession countries), for example, Turkey and some North African and Middle Eastern countries.

The Southern African Development Community (SADC) created the SADC P3 Network, housed with the SADC Development Finance Resource Center (DFRC). The SADC P3's main objective is to strengthen the capacity of PPP practitioners for defining, managing, and implementing PPP policies, programs, and projects by learning from each other and by harmonizing processes, institutions, and policies across the region. Deutsche Gesellschaft für Internationale Zusammenarbeit (German Agency for International Cooperation; GIZ), the bilateral donor, has provided funding to recruit a PPP specialist for two years to develop the work program of the P3 Network and to identify funding and resources. Country representatives have been appointed by Senior Treasury Officials from the SADC Member States. The World Bank Institute (WBI) and the EPEC are functioning as knowledge partners for the P3 Network. As part of the work program, the following activities will be undertaken:

- Four working groups are under way or planned for: Policies/Institutions; Procurement of PPPs; Health Sector PPPs; and Municipal PPPs. These groups will develop common approaches or recommended solutions to be adopted at the country level; they were chosen in consultation with the P3 Network members
- Private sector forum—regular interaction with the private sector
- Structured learning and other capacity building events.

One final example is in Central America, where the WBI is coordinating with the International Finance Corporation (IFC) to provide a regional solution to improving capacities for PPPs by working with the Central American Bank for Economic Integration (CABEI). As part of this, the WBI and the IFC are providing support on capacity building and transaction design, respectively. The goal is for CABEI to be able to provide a convening point for PPP units and line agencies and to develop its own expertise to help in transactions and projects.

It is important to note that in none of the cases in box 3.2 does the regional initiative substitute for the role that national agencies have in their own PPP programs. For example, while national PPP units usually have regulatory, oversight, or approval powers, a PPP Resource Center such as the EPEC does not. It is instead focused more on convening, coordinating, and capacity building. There are, of course, differences in the examples described above—for example, the EPEC has nearly 20 professional staff and therefore can deliver a large volume of advisory services to the countries it serves. In contrast, the SADC P3 Network will, for the foreseeable future, have a relatively small core level of support and will rely on external support for delivering services to member countries. In Central America, an important focus is strengthening the capacities of the CABEI so it can help individual countries develop PPP programs as well as provide a subregional focal point for capacity building.

Possible roles for a PPP Resource Center in building capacities for PPPs in Partner States: Based on the recommendations from the regional workshops and country consultations undertaken to date, five areas have been identified where the EAC can play an active role in the PPP space. To do so, it will need to create a focal point or resource center with appropriate resources to properly implement any functions it would undertake. These are summarised in figure 3.1 below. It should be stressed that it will not be practical to undertake all of these activities initially, and there are some that the EAC may choose not to address at all. It is also critical that any activities undertaken by a PPP Resource Center do not conflict with what national PPP units and/or line agencies do in the PPP space in line with their mandates developed under national policies, legislation, and regulations.

Training and Knowledge Exchange

Although the Partner States are pursuing capacity building programs and other activities to strengthen their frameworks and institutions, there is scope for the EAC to add value to this through the following activities:

- Convening regular meetings of PPP units and line agencies working on PPP to discuss areas of common interest and exchange experiences. This would assist

Figure 3.1 Possible Functions of an EAC PPP Resource Center

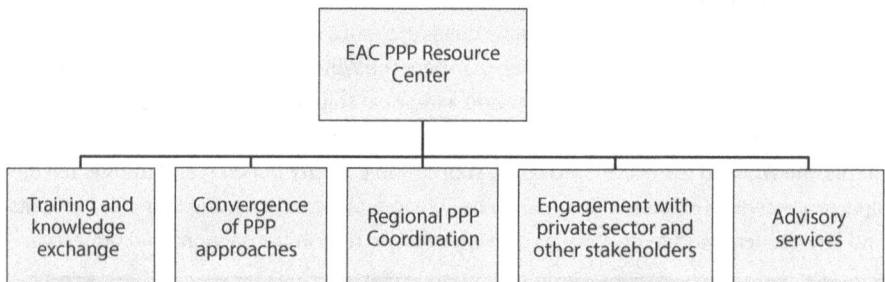

Source: World Bank.
Note: EAC = East African Community; PPP = Public-Private Partnership.

in keeping the agencies current on the PPP projects and initiatives being undertaken by all Partner States, and would allow individuals in the PPP units to follow up afterwards on particular issues

- Identifying training needs and coordinating these where economies of scale would make a regional approach more efficient than a national one
- Developing databases on PPP projects and analytical publications and reports from the Partner State
- Coordinating knowledge exchange from PPP practitioners from outside the EAC; for example, connecting the EAC to other regional networks (including the SADC P3N, the EPEC, and others), as well as using knowledge partners such as the World Bank.

Harmonizing the EAC PPP market—Working to converge Approaches on PPPs

As noted above, all the EAC Partner State markets are relatively small in global or even regional terms (for example, compared to those in South Africa and Nigeria). Foreign investors are often not interested in individual projects in small new markets because of high entry costs. However, they are more likely to invest if there is a larger pipeline of projects. More projects increase their chances of winning bids and make the market entry worthwhile. A harmonized EAC PPP market would potentially offer such a pipeline, because even if some countries have only a few projects, as a region they will constitute a significant market.

Convergence would, at least initially, have to come from an organic process of PPP units reviewing good practices from within and outside the EAC and working together on specific projects and issues to develop approaches that all could replicate on a voluntary basis. Convergence benefits could be considerable. Harmonization of frameworks would effectively create an EAC-wide market for PPPs, rather than five smaller national markets. Private companies interested in PPPs in the region would need to be familiar with just one approach to PPP procurement, rather than learning several approaches practiced in the different Partner States. Such a harmonization exercise would need to consider:

- **Selection of PPPs**: Legislation at the EAC level could create a process for determining when a project is eligible for selection as a PPP, with some standardization on feasibility studies and criteria for selection of projects;
- **Procurement of PPPs**: There is no common standard or procedure for procurement within the EAC, whether relating to regional PPPs or PPPs within Partner States. It is possible that in time, beyond the type of procedural "transparency" proposed in the above coordination section, general public procurement may be subject to the wider harmonization initiative being carried out in the context of the ongoing EAC effort to build a common market. Given that procurement of PPPs is a discrete topic from general procurement, it could be addressed by the EAC as part of a separate exercise;

- **Development of standardized contract clauses and or documents**: Sometime in the future, it might be appropriate for the EAC to develop standardized bidding documents/some standardized clauses for regional projects. It might also make sense for the EAC to develop model approaches for national level projects where standard approaches might encourage efficiencies.

Coordination Role for Regional PPPs

The EAC could play a role in advancing the PPP agenda at both the Partner State and Regional level through one or more of the following activities:

- **Project development:** The EAC's role could extend to coordination of tender processes in regional PPP projects (which is already taking place with respect to donor grant-funded infrastructure projects such as the one-stop border post initiative) and development of feasibility studies for regional PPP projects. In some cases, the EAC already plays this role in infrastructure projects. For example, the Council decision EAC/CM13/DC11 authorizes the Secretariat to act as the executing agency of the study on behalf of Tanzania and Kenya for the Arusha–Holili–Taveta-Voi and Tanga–Horohoro–Malindi road project studies and investment planning as required by the African Development Bank (AfDB) in consideration of the US$5.5 million support for the two projects. The role of the EAC could even extend to coordination of the development of bidding documents for regional projects—to ensure segments of regional projects in Partner States are coordinated and consistent and come to market/are completed within the same timeframe.
- **Implementer/project manager of regional PPPs:** The EAC could potentially act as an agent for relevant Partner States in implementing and project managing regional PPPs. There was consensus that if and when (and it is not foreseen in the near future) EAC were to take on this role, it would likely be on a case-by-case basis and would be under the framework of an agreement between the relevant Partner States (that is, bilateral/tripartite agreement) rather than under the umbrella of the Treaty.
- **Procurement of regional PPPs:** While it is clear from stakeholder feedback that it is currently too early to try to develop procurement processes for regional PPP projects, it is recommended that there be general principles of procurement set out in the draft policy and that this be considered in the medium to long term as a possible mechanism for facilitating regional PPP projects. Coordination of procurement of regional infrastructure projects is currently complicated by the need to follow different procurement procedures for each segment of a project located in a Partner State (unless it is procured for a multilateral or bilateral development agency funded project, in which case the rules of that agency are likely to apply). If the EAC were able to reach consensus on and develop one procedure for procurement of regional PPP projects, projects might be better coordinated. It would also give investors into the region confidence in the process to be followed.

Providing Bilateral Advisory Services on PPP to EAC Partner States

Partner States also expressed interest in having the EAC develop resources to provide advisory services to them either directly or by co-opting peers from another Partner State with a view to helping them implement their own national PPP programs. Fulfilling this mandate would require considerably more technical resources than would be implied for convening and capacity building activities and, even were the EAC to try to implement this, it would be important not to offer what is already available from the advisory market.

Priority areas for advisory services might be on program/policy support and helping PPP units to define consultancy needs and/or to steer consultants in cases where the public sector lacks the necessary skills. A critical area might be in assisting PPP units or line agencies to manage transaction advisors to get the desired outcomes. Ideally, the experience from such assignments could be aggregated and made available again to other EAC countries facing similar challenges. A more modest form of advisory support would be to establish a Helpdesk which could give rapid responses to immediate questions, or redirect these questions to other members of the center and/or Partner States with relevant expertise.

Engaging with the Private Sector and Stakeholders

The EAC PPP Resource Center could play an important role in providing a neutral forum for dialogue between the public and private sectors and allow discussions to take place that might be more difficult at the national level. In addition, organizing regional investor conferences may allow a larger critical mass of investors to be gathered together. There is obviously a link between this and the activities that the EAC might take to develop more harmonized approaches. The EAC PPP Resource Center should also reach out to the advisory community (which needs to be familiar with the topics being discussed by the public sector with regard to PPPs) and the financial institutions that need to familiarize themselves with the necessary structures and develop adequate financial instruments. In addition, an EAC PPP Resource Center can also be a vehicle through which PPP units and line agencies dialogue with other stakeholders. While dialogue should also take place at the national level, an EAC forum can help civil society and parliamentarians learn from experiences in PPP implementation from across the community, leading to a more informed discussion.

Locating and resourcing a PPP Resource Center in the EAC: Were the EAC to establish a PPP Resource Center, it would be important to consider the following:

- **Practical focus:** There has to be a strong emphasis on the practical aspects related to getting PPP projects prepared and financed—there would be little value added from locating the center in a university which would have an academic focus and would be of less assistance to PPP practitioners in the Partner State agencies.
- **Center scope:** Resources have to be commensurate with the scale of the tasks, both in terms of volume and quality; for example, if the EAC wishes to have a

PPP Center that can provide advisory support or peer review to Partner States, then individuals in the center must have the necessary expertise. In terms of the overall volume of resources, there is clearly a difference between a "network lite" model which restricts itself to a small program of capacity building and knowledge exchange between PPP units, and a Resource Center which sponsors and produces joint work on issues of interest, and a true regional center which has sufficient personnel to undertake peer review and promote and support regional PPP projects via managing processes and resources to support these.

- **Complementarity:** If the EAC is planning to implement funding mechanisms, including a Project Development Facility (PDF) or Viability Gap Facility (VGF), it might make sense to bundle the management structure for these along with a PPP Center focused on capacity building. Although these funds might have their own separate oversight mechanisms, the fact that they would be tied into supporting PPPs and would require approval and review processes means that it might be efficient and effective to house under the same roof any resources advising PPP units more generally on PPP processes. At the same time, it is important that there are no conflicts of interest. For example, if the PPP Center were to play an important role in the procurement of some PPP projects (perhaps regional ones), locating it within a financing agency might lead to a conflict of interest.

For all of these reasons, the optimal place for locating a PPP Resource Center is the East African Development Bank (EADB), where it could be a joint unit with the EAC Secretariat, with staff seconded from the EADB. This would have the advantage of linking it to the policy and convening power of the EAC as well as the financial skills and perspective of the EADB. For the reasons outlined earlier, there does not appear to be an existing EAC organization with broad enough oversight, nor does it seem appropriate to locate the Center in an institution of higher learning. Participants at the Experts' Workshop and the country consultations endorsed the option of placing a Resource Center at the EADB, given the latter's close links to project financing and the need for the center to have a practical focus.

PPP Financing: Issues and Options

There may also be scope for the EAC to play a proactive role in the development and financing of specific projects; for example, through project development funds or financing support for PPP projects. Over the course of this work, consideration was given to the potential of three different instruments: (i) a long-term local currency debt financing facility; (ii) a Viability Gap Facility; and (iii) a project development facility. Each is discussed in more detail next.

Long-term Local Currency Debt Financing Facility: As noted earlier, with the exception of Kenya, none of the capital markets within the EAC provides significantly longer-term domestic debt financing. This constrains prospects for financial close, due to the existence of risks such as currency and term mismatches where they cannot be adequately hedged. In this context, consideration was given to possible regional solutions to compensate for the EAC's current capital market limitations, such as the provision of commercially based, longer-term, local-denominated liquidity to prospective PPP financiers and operators. This funding could come in the form of an on-lending line of credit and/or partial guarantees.

While there was wide concurrence across both public and financial sector stakeholders on the need for longer-term local currency debt financing, arranging this on a regional level poses a number of challenges that, over the short and medium term, suggest that this is an initiative to revisit at a later date. There are three main considerations behind this conclusion. First, the EAC will need to determine more clearly the pipeline that would be eligible for long-term debt financing support (including a definition of eligible projects). This is required to provide some estimate of the prospective amount of funding required for such a financing facility. Second, unlike the VGF, which would most probably be funded through grant contributions, a long-term debt financing facility is likely to attract principally interest-bearing foreign currency allocations which—if these funds are to be used to provide domestic currency financing—will entail a foreign exchange risk consideration that will need to be addressed. Covering these risks will likely require additional sovereign government exposure. Finally, it would be advisable to monitor progress and the project track record of the evolving enabling environments in Partner States before establishing a financial instrument that will require returns on investment that will be particularly sensitive to the effectiveness of these newly developing PPP framework environments.

At a later point, if there is further consideration of the merits of a regional financing facility as outlined above, the question of where to house such a facility will need to be addressed. One candidate subject to continuing institutional improvements and performance related to balance sheet, governance, and operational capacities would be the EADB. Based on the analysis done to date (see appendix F of this report), for the EADB to be sufficiently prepared to take on such a role, it would need to recruit specialized project finance capacity and staff to perform the primary additional responsibility; that is, appraising the quality and appropriateness of candidate participating financial intermediaries.

Viability Gap Facility (VGF): The "regional" (for example, cross-border) segments of some infrastructure may not be commercially viable, but nevertheless can have significant economic benefits, spillover, or other externalities which from a regional rationale merit capture. Where this is the case, a VGF focused particularly on support to upfront additional capital costs needed to realize regional connectivity could play an important incentivizing role and enable a regional project to come to market.

Current estimates of the financing shortfall for "regionally" significant transport infrastructure that could attract PPP investment are US$2–3 billion out of a total estimated US$4.2–6 billion investment requirement.[3] In many instances, private financing will not be sufficient to fund these infrastructure investments. A VGF can play a key role in bridging the commercial gap between a project's cost and what the private sector is willing to mobilize. If the VGF allocation is made on the basis of a competitive bidding process, it adds a further market-based cost-effectiveness discipline to public investment funds. It will be important for the EAC Secretariat, in cooperation with Partner States, to identify some first-mover transactions that can be bid out for VGF allocations. In addition, these initial projects identified for VGF support will need to provide a reasonably high likelihood of reaching market, which in turn is a function of the capital cost, revenue potential, and political risks that will determine commercial attractiveness. Box 3.3 provides more detail on the rationale and prospective design features for a VGF focused on fostering regional PPP transactions.

Box 3.3 Rational for and Design of a Viability Gap Facility

Why a Viability Gap Facility? Given demand estimates and assessments of willingness and ability to pay across many of the infrastructure sectors in emerging and developing markets, it is anticipated that—with the exception of telecommunications—much of a region's core infrastructure will continue to require substantial public sector investment over the coming phase of development. The capital cost and revenue structures of many infrastructure developments will preclude wholly commercial financing solutions and more specifically, the investment costs to capture "cross-border" benefits may not have sufficient cost-benefit rates of return to mobilize national government financing, given other demands on limited capital budget headroom. A VGF designed to finance this "regional" "viability gap" could be a key part of the overall regional infrastructure financing solution. The VGF could provide upfront funding to cover a certain amount of the project cost associated with the cross-border aspects of a regional investment. The required capitalization level of the VGF would need to be determined on the basis of estimates drawn from the projected pipeline of projects to be financed.

VGF Allocations: A VGF allocation to a prospective PPP would be based on a detailed upfront assessment, including a determination as to whether an investment is a regional priority and conforms to the criteria established by the EAC for eligibility. This will require a cost-benefit analysis and a "value for money" determination of whether the project is suitable for a PPP structure; that is, if a PPP arrangement could deliver the investment at an overall lower cost and better service quality through the involvement of private operators and financiers versus a strictly public financing arrangement. This upstream investment appraisal work is a key first step in determining the public merit of an investment, the PPP rationale, and in laying the foundation for the detailed PPP project development, structuring, and financing that will then follow.

The Competitive Aspect of a VGF: The other important feature of a VGF is the competitive process it utilizes and the additional cost discipline that this introduces to the VGF allocation exercise. VGF funding should be competitively awarded to the bidder who submits the proposal for the lowest VGF allocation consistent with the technical, operational, market, and other specifications laid out in the VGF bid documents. Given this market approach and the intent to make the VGF available for more than one sector, the VGF would need to be administered through a suitably technically qualified central agency. This serves to ensure that the funds available under a VGF go to the highest priority and most cost-effective proposals. In the case of a regional VGF, the funds would be provided from the EAC to the lead government agency managing the regional project for payment to the successful concessionaire/project sponsor.

Based on discussions with key Partner State public and private sector stake-holders, together with the current assessment of the region's financial and capital sector markets and the recent decision of the EAC to establish an EAC Development Fund (EACDF),[4] initial consideration should be given to the intro-duction of a VGF window. This instrument would be well suited to support the objectives of the EACDF. The EACDF Policy Framework indicates that a key objective of the fund is "to support development projects with a regional out-look" (refer to Article 1.3ii), which the proposed VGF would exactly serve. The proposed instrument would also represent concrete steps towards the first objec-tive of "establishing a legal and institutional framework for mainstreaming sup-port…" from the development community (refer to Article 1.3i). These facilities could also play a critical role towards the objective to "involve the private sector in development initiatives…."

To complete the further due diligence to determine more accurately the ratio-nale and demand for a VGF, the EAC will need to confirm its current proposed definition of "regional PPPs" and develop a suitable pipeline of projects for pro-spective funding. Additional attention will need to be paid to the set criteria for screening regional projects and conducting the proper analysis needed to ensure that the proposed regional project is best suited for a PPP, such as a VfM analy-sis, and is part of both the regional and Partner State development plans. At a minimum, this project screening should be based on the following parameters:

- Completion of some initial analysis but requiring further PPP-specific work
- A clear mandate for the EAC to assist in project development and structuring
- Projects, whether with a cross-border or a more specific national focus but at all times with clear potential regional benefits
- Projects that only involve existing EAC Partner States

While it has not yet been possible to undertake a more in-depth assessment of prospective pipeline projects, there are some key considerations regarding what types of projects to target. The selection of initial projects on which to estimate the initial size of the VGF will be critical to the longer-term credibility of the mechanism. Projects that involve high upfront capital investment (for example, greenfield standard gauge railway initiatives) and local currency reve-nue base (for example, toll road projects) will pose larger risks. Considering specifically the political and sequencing risks, projects for which there is an established regional approach (for example, Lake Victoria or Regional Power Interconnectors) or where there is substantial revenue potential (for example, oil and gas pipelines) offer the more likely candidates.

Once the targeted set of first-mover projects are selected, the EAC, together with the relevant Partner States, should undertake outreach to the international development community to sensitize and mobilize interest in financing, making a case for prioritizing funding to a regional VGF, based on a solid development and economic rationale, and reinforced with evidence of strong political commit-ment (for example, an approved policy and a clearly established pipeline of projects agreed at highest levels) and institutional capacity to implement. It is possible that the VGF will not be funded at levels to meet all demand. Clear signals will need to be given to ensure—particularly in the start-up phase of such a facility—that prospective sponsors know when and how much funding is reliably in place to support projects. All approved allocations, which may well be disbursed over a two- to three-year period, would require 100 percent provisioning. This will also necessitate a well-sequenced process of VGF replenishments to maintain the availability of funds for upcoming pipeline projects.

A number of factors come into play when considering the feasibility of establishing a regional VGF. This encompasses both political and institutional considerations. A VGF would need to be publicly funded. This implies either government contributions or international grants and concessionary resources. In discussing these different financing instruments and sources, Partner State interlocutors cautioned that the EAC should not be in competition with national PPP fund-raising efforts—particularly since a number of Partner States are looking to develop their own VGF mechanisms. Similarly, in terms of international donor support for a regional VGF, to what extent would this initiative compete for scarce donor funds available for national infrastructure initiatives? To systematically address these trade-offs, the development of a viable policy framework with full Partner State buy-in, founded on specifically measurable PPP outcomes, is important. It will be a critical signal to prospective funding sources as to how they should prioritize allocations.

In addition to these factors, there are the ones relating to institutional capacity to effectively manage a VGF. This is both a design and implementation challenge. In terms of design, the following features are identified for consideration:

- **Institutional requirements, roles, and responsibilities:** The VGF should be structured such that a suitable institution of the EAC has overall fiduciary and performance oversight of the mechanism. This EAC institution should oversee the application and award process, subject to eligibility and performance criteria, and fulfill monitoring and reporting functions.
- **Partner State demand driven:** Specific applications for VGF funding should be submitted by Partner States. In those instances where more than one state is involved, the designated "Lead" Partner State could undertake this responsibility.
- **Project eligibility:** This would be based on a "positive list" of candidate projects as agreed between the EAC and Partner States. This positive list would be based on an upstream prefeasibility assessment of the regional impact of candidate investments. This assessment approach would take into consideration: (i) conformity to the requirements for "regional" project designation, in line with the policy; and (ii) the cost-benefit estimate (to the extent that it can be estimated) including the scope, level, and timing of for the specific "regional" aspect of the infrastructure; (iii) the feasibility of realizing the regional benefit.
- **VGF ceiling:** Agreement will need to be reached on what share of total project financing could be provided by the regional VGF facility and the extent to which this can be additional to any planned national public investment/ VGF contributions.

To make best use of scarce technical expertise and foster ownership, the VGF mechanism should build on existing regional and national capacities and complement this as required with contracted expertise. In this respect, it is proposed that the EAC Secretariat undertake an assessment of the following issues and options:

- **Links with EACDF:** The pros and cons of integrating a VGF instrument into the evolving design and implementing arrangements for the EACDF should be investigated.
- **Apex institution options:** There are essentially three options available for consideration:
  - Administration by an existing institution of the EAC. The best suited for this role, albeit after capacity building requirements are first addressed, would be the EADB.
  - Outsourcing to a suitable private sector entity for daily management with oversight from a key EAC institution such as the EADB. This option could provide a short-to-medium-term solution, until a portfolio track record is established and an EAC institution develops the capacity to take on the responsibility directly.
  - Recruitment of a "Fund Manager," possibly from a suitably qualified, regionally based institution, with project finance expertise and a proven track record.
- **Standardized documentation:** Utilize the project structuring documents prepared by the Partner State(s) as the basis for assessing VGF proposals, after ensuring key standardized features are included in the documents to facilitate the VGF appraisal work.
- **Core competence requirements:** Ensure that the EAC institution responsible for the overall oversight has core project finance capabilities or at least a business environment within its institution that would foster and sustain its development over time.

Project Development Facility (PDF): PPP project preparation from preappraisal through to structured transaction can entail significant costs. In discussion with Partner States, it was noted that funding sources to finance these costs are not easily accessible, although it was acknowledged that there a number of underutilized options currently available from different sources. One action would be to ensure a better stocktaking and increased awareness of available funds, as well as improvements to enable more ready access to these funds by EAC countries. Beyond this, the provision of PDF funds to specifically finance the regional aspects of feasibility and structuring work which may not otherwise be factored into a project design as Partner States focus on the national priorities and/or seek to conserve on project costs was considered an area of potential additionality to be further investigated.

Financing the upfront due diligence costs for assessing and preparing a project for market often lies beyond the reach of governments and institutions in the region. This increases susceptibility to unsolicited bids which, not being subject to a competitive process and often not based on sufficiently thorough economic and financial analysis, can more easily result in poorly designed and insufficiently cost-effective projects governed by ill-prepared contracts. Detailed financial modeling is a scarce and insufficiently applied expertise by public institutions responsible for assessing and deploying public funds. Establishing an instrument that would finance these upstream activities could have a significant impact across all aspects of the project's economic robustness, cost effectiveness, and contract quality.

A facility dedicated to finance due diligence on regional projects compliant with EAC-authorized eligibility criteria would serve to provide some additional momentum to the development of these projects. As with the VGF, the eventual synergies and impact effects will depend critically on getting projects to market. The PDF should be established as a funding mechanism rather than a technical assistance service. Partner States would be encouraged to submit applications for PDF allocations to projects with eligible regional relevance. The allocations would be transferred to the Partner State/Lead State to manage, with specialized economic consultants/transactions advisors recruited to undertake the work.

In determining where to house the PDF, where the roles and responsibilities would include administering the fund—both from a fiduciary and a development monitoring perspective—it would be advantageous if the selected institution had project finance expertise and a conducive business environment. This could also be obtained by contracting out the mechanism on a management fee basis, reporting to a relevant agency of the EAC. Where the management of the PDF is contracted out, it will be important to set out clear guidelines to ensure that potential conflicts of interest are avoided/mitigated; for example, cases where PDF funds are directed to projects for which the PDF manager also has a commercial interest.

Notes

1. Art 7(b) of the Treaty.
2. Art 89.
3. This estimate was derived from preliminary project cost analysis provided in the "Corridor Diagnostic of the East Africa," a report prepared by Nathan and Associates, submitted by the EAC to the Task Coordination Group in April 2011 and project profiles included in report prepared for the Tripartite and Intergovernmental Authority on Development (IGAD) Investment Conference, September 28–29, 2011.
4 The EAC Secretariat has in drafts (dated March 2011) both a "Policy Framework on the Establishment of the East African Community Development Fund" and a "Protocol on the Establishment of the East African Community Development Fund." These will provide basis for ongoing dialogue around the rationale and institutional arrangements for a prospective Financial Intermediary Loan (FIL) and/or VGF type mechanism for regional PPPs.

CHAPTER 4

Conclusion: Key Elements of a Strategic Business Plan

Key Criteria for a Strategic Business Plan

At this point in time, the East African Community (EAC) and its Partner States are considering whether to proceed with a regional Public-Private Partnership (PPP) policy initiative. Policies principally address the "What" and the "Why," as set out in chapter 3 of this report. Questions of "How" and "When" are the issues more usually addressed in a Strategic Business Plan (SBP). In preparing an SBP, the key challenges are to ensure delivery and outcome. The former entails an assessment of institutional delivery capacity and the latter, measurability. In addition, budgets and timeframes need to be established. What follows is an outline of a proposed SBP addressing these different considerations. In arriving at optimal institutional arrangements, outcome objectives, budget requirements, and timeframe parameters, attention needs to be paid to issues of feasibility, sustainability, synergies, and impact as more fully portrayed in box 4.1.

Box 4.1 Developing a Strategic Business Plan

Criteria	Variable	Description of variable
Feasibility	Political will and institutional capacity	Does the political commitment for the policy actions and initiatives exist?
		Can winners and losers be identified? Losers compensated?
		Beyond the reform champions, is there sufficient institutional capability to implement?
	Sequencing	Are there sequencing considerations?
		Do certain measures better suit shorter- or longer-term timeframes?

box continues next page

Box 4.1 Conclusion—Key Elements of a Strategic Business Plan *(continued)*

Criteria	Variable	Description of variable
Synergies and Impact		Do the planned initiatives have the potential to catalyze a broader alliance for reform to follow through or scale up? Three elements by which to assess this are:
	Demonstration	(i) **Demonstration effects:** Does the initiative offer quick wins and tangible impacts to lock in commitment and maintain momentum?
	Linkages	(ii) **Linkages:** Are there links to other stakeholders and capacity to *scale up reforms* or positive *spillovers* to other areas (for example, where institutions created for one reform can apply newly gained expertise and champion related or other reforms)? If so, there are *knock-on effects* where a reform initiative raises awareness and appetite to deal with related reforms?
	Measurement	(iii) **Measurement:** Can the policy impact be credibly measured? Do objectives and broadly accepted benchmarks exist?
Sustainability/ Cost	Budget and other resource implications	Are there significant upfront or recurrent cost or revenue gain/loss considerations?
		Is the reform financially sustainable?
		Can gaps in institutional capacities essential for success be addressed in parallel with implementing the reform program?

Establishing Measurable Policy Outcomes

For a policy to be successful, it ideally needs to build momentum and deliver some early tangible results. This can be seen as a function of demonstration effects, linkages to other stakeholders, and measurability. In the context of the regional PPP policy, it is recommended that the EAC Secretariat, working in consultation with key representatives of the EAC Partner States, identify and target for development two or three priority regional PPPs that would be taken to market. This would represent a clear measure of policy success, serve as a very tangible vehicle with which to collaborate with other critical stakeholders—both Partner States, the broader private sector and the donor community—and provide an accountability against which the relevance of the policy can be ascertained.

It is well recognized that selecting "priority" projects is not straightforward. As noted earlier, it is will be critical that these projects are selected with due regard to their feasibility and potential to satisfy the other key criteria of synergy and impact. Projects that provide positive demonstration effects, link in other key stakeholders, and have clear milestones and measurable outcomes will all serve to give credibility and generate momentum for the policy.

Creation of a Task Force

Currently, the capacity in the EAC Secretariat and its affiliated institutions is fully extended. In addition to current mandates and workloads, there are additional expertise limitations that would inhibit existing entities and staff from dedicating the level of time and effort required to complete the detailed preparation of a prospective EAC regional PPP policy and undertake the subsequent implementation responsibilities. It is therefore recommended that the implementation of a regional PPP framework be undertaken through the establishment of a Task Force, as recommended by the participants at the Experts' Workshop. Such a Task Force would also represent a key step towards ensuring policy "sustainability" over the critical next phase of final policy preparation and the initial stages of implementation. It was recognized that the Task Force mechanism has been particularly useful in developing the single currency initiative, for instance, as it enabled Partner States to work together, while being accountable to the Council for clear outputs and timetable. The Task Force could be facilitated by a PPP Resource Center (see the following section), and it is expected that its membership would include PPP units from the EAC.

The creation of an effective Task Force is essential to getting the regional PPP agenda up and running. To be effective, it must have legitimacy (by securing the backing of all Partner States), and must also be able to move quickly and get things done. The Task Force will play a key role in moving many of the recommendations of this report forward. In particular it could:

- Create a regional PPP pipeline, including two or three pilot projects that can be used for demonstration effects. These should be chosen for their feasibility and could be smaller projects. The emphasis should be on getting some successful transactions done. The Task Force could also be involved in making sure these projects go through to financial close.
- Begin to build the Resource Center by identifying capacity building needs at the EAC level and recruiting staff for a phased development of its capacity, commencing with the "network lite" option.
- Further investigate the possibility of regional PPP funding facilities, including identifying donors and the institution that will administer the funds, possibly the East African Development Bank (EADB).

In support of these recommendations, the scope of work for the Task Force,[1] as agreed at the July 18–19, 2012 Validation Workshop, was identified as follows:
1. Develop the regional policy framework.
2. Identify, in consultation with Partner States, a pipeline of at least two regional PPP projects.

3. Consider PPP financing options and their development, including the Project Development Facility (PDF) and Viability Gap Facility (VGF).
4. Develop the medium-term plan for a PPP Resource Center for the EAC.
5. Finalize the SBP, including key milestones for (1)–(4) above.

The Task Force requires experienced individuals with the authority to get things done at the individual country level. Existing PPP Units should be a good source of Task Force members, as they will have the relevant experience as well as the networks needed to get things done. It is important, however, that this regional exercise does not undermine progress being made at the national level. Any recruitment for the Task Force should be done with the full cooperation of individual Partner States.

Budgetary Requirements

Budgetary resources will need to be deployed to ensure sustainability of policy implementation. This can be determined for an initial shorter-term (one to two years) period and then over a longer term (two to five years). Given the costs in properly resourcing this and the still relatively nascent state of national PPP markets, it makes sense for the EAC to take a gradual approach to developing a focal point for PPPs at the EAC level. At the consultation workshops in Nairobi (August 2011) and Arusha (October 2011), the "network lite" option was identified as one that could provide an initial focal point in the EAC on PPPs supporting the recommended Task Force while national systems are being established.

Short-term budget requirements: This would encompass, but not be limited to:

- The Task Force, which in turn will be dependent on its mandate, functionality, work plan responsibilities, and expertise requirement
- Initial Resource Center costs, particularly for the "network lite" option
- Initial capacity building support for core EAC institutions with regional PPP policy responsibilities—such as the EADB and the EAC Secretariat
- Preliminary PDF requirements for upstream work on the identification of targeted two to three lead regional PPP transactions
- Budget for "due diligence," for instance, to assess the institutional options for the VGF/PDF.

The scope of work over a two-year period would be for the "network lite" option to support the PPP Task Force in the following areas:

- Identify immediate capacity building and training needs at the EAC level, and develop a resource plan by working with bilateral and multilateral donors to deliver these.
- Organize an annual event involving the private sector on regional PPP programs; this could be done in collaboration with existing forums discussing regional infrastructure.

- Coordinate the Task Force and assist in the fulfillment of its terms of references, which includes detailed scoping of the regional PPP Resource Center functions and resource requirements.
- Convene working groups consisting of the PPP Units and other relevant agencies to work on two to three key topics that would provide a foundation for convergence on key issues. The precise topics should be identified by the Task Force but examples could include (i) work to develop standard contracts for one or two sectors with high replication potential; (ii) key aspects of procurement (for example, dealing with unsolicited projects); and (iii) approaches to managing fiscal costs.

Longer-term budget requirements: Some of the key activities to be supported over the more extended period would be:

- Capacity building program for the selected regional PPP policy "implementing agency;" for example, the EADB
- Mobilization of initial funding for the PDF and VGF to meet approved pipeline requirements
- Establishment of a fully scoped regional PPP Resource Center.

Over the longer term, the budget requirements for a properly functioning PPP Resource Center could be considerable. A detailed budget estimate was not developed here, in part because the exact budget depends on the level and range of services desired by the Partner States. However, at a minimum, the center can expect to house a limited number of qualified professionals who can cover the range of topics discussed earlier. It is essential for these professionals to have skills related to infrastructure and finance. It might also be possible to use secondees to the EAC from donor countries as part of the more junior staff. But for this to be a credible resource to Partner States, there can be no shortcuts in terms of putting in place experienced staff who can provide some value added to the country-level PPP agencies.

Note

1. The detailed terms of reference for the Task Force, as agreed by all Partner State representatives to the July 18–19, 2012 Validation Workshop, are included as appendix D of the signed Report of the Workshop.

PPP Country Framework Templates

Burundi

Policy, legal, and regulatory framework	
Public-Private Partnership (PPP policies)	The PPP framework is very nascent. This is under the Public-Private Dialogue (PPD) Secretariat in second vice president's office which is where economic and development matters are housed. A study is being undertaken by the PPD Secretariat (see below)—supported by a recently approved World Bank Private Sector Development (PSD) project—to look at the formulation of a PPP framework.
PPP legislation	The legal framework in the country is very complicated (over 200 permissions required to construct a building). The East African Community (EAC) presents an opportunity in that if Burundi realigns itself to EAC standard approaches/laws in many areas, then it can greatly simplify its current regulatory regime. The World Bank has recently assisted in the preparation of a draft of PPP law.
Institutional structure	
Political/strategic leadership	A presidential decree established a framework for dialogue and coordination between the public and private sectors (PPD) in 2008. This has very broad objectives and is not in any way specific to PPPs or basic services. It has a General Assembly (headed by second vice president), an Executive Board, and Technical Groups (for specific issues) composed of members of the public and private sectors.
Allocation of responsibilities in PPP process (including in contract management and regulation)	**Public-Private Dialogue Secretariat**—The Secretariat, constituted in November 2010 and reporting to the second vice president, is responsible for the PPP agenda. It is not presently working on PPPs, however. The decree and overall structure of the PPD Secretariat indicate that it would be an appropriate forum for mobilizing discussion on a PPP program/framework. The Secretariat does not currently anticipate housing any of the advisory, monitoring/enforcement, or gatekeeper roles ordinarily associated with PPP Units.
	There is a privatization agency (Service Charge des Enterprises Publiques [Burundi] SCEP) that has oversight of public enterprises and is a technical service unit for undertaking privatizations, which are overseen by a committee of ministries. There is a privatization law which sets the overall framework, and SCEP was established by a decree.

table continues next page

Policy, legal, and regulatory framework	
	Insofar as some privatizations are similar to PPPs in that they have involved some form of management contract of different duration, rather than outright sale to the private sector (examples include the Bujumbura port, and a textiles company), there may be PPP expertise within SCEP that would provide the basis for some PPP Unit functions to be delivered initially from SCEP.
Existing infrastructure PPP operations	Bujumbura has limited experience with PPPs, but the Bujumbura port management contract is still in place after 10 years. There is, by some accounts, considerable experience with private provision of education and health and this could be a good springboard for PPPs in these sectors. There are seven private universities and a number of faith-based schools and hospitals.
	Power: Lack of electricity capacity was a serious constraint to developing mining resources. The government is actively working on studies for both national level and regional level projects, all of them hydroelectric plants. The bigger regional projects include Ruzomo Falls, where they will interconnect with the system (not recommended as a PPP) and Ruzeri 3 and 4 (3 is 147 megawatts and US$581 million, 4 would be 287 megawatts, but no estimated cost was available at time of preparing this report). The broader sector reform allows for the creation of a regulator in the power sector, but this has not happened yet.
	Transport: In terms of PPPs, one of the priorities is the extension of the central rail corridor. The portion in Burundi was estimated to cost US$1.5 billion (portions in Rwanda and Tanzania are US$800 million and US$700 million, respectively).
	The government is also investigating the development of Bujumbura as a regional port, including connecting via lake transport to Mpulungu in Zambia.

Source: World Bank.

Kenya

Policy, legal, and regulatory framework	
PPP policies	PPP Policy approved by the Cabinet at the beginning of 2012
PPP legislation	Kenyan Public Procurement and Disposal (PPP) Regulations 2009 (PPP Regulations), issued under the Public Procurement and Disposal Act 2005, were the principal legal instruments for PPPs. There is now a new Public Private Partnerships Act, passed by parliament in December 2012. The procurement of PPPs will henceforth be managed under the PPP Act, and it is intended that the Public Procurement and Disposal Act 2005 will not apply to PPPs.
	The bill provides a broad definition of PPPs that would cover operation contracts through to concessions and land swaps, and could be interpreted to cover management contracts.
Implementing regulations	PPP regulations and guidelines were scheduled to be developed late 2012, particularly covering in more detail the Project Facilitation Fund (section 53), project identification, and rules and procedures for submission of bids and opening of envelopes.

table continues next page

Policy, legal, and regulatory framework	
Contracts—standard terms, and so on	PPP Bill sets out minimum contractual obligations that PPP agreements will be required to include. PPP Committee is responsible for approving standardized bid documents.
Institutional structure	
Political/strategic leadership	**Public Private Partnership Committee (PPPC)** to be established under the PPP Act comprising principal secretaries from relevant departments (Principal Secretary for Finance is Chair) and four nonpublic servant experts. This replaces the PPP Steering Committee established under the PPP Regulations.
	The PPPC is responsible for general policy on PPPs; approval of PPPs; authorization of allocation of funds from Project Facilitation Fund; approval of PPP standards, guidelines, and procedures and development of standardized bid documents; championing the PPP process and promoting PPPs and capacity building; approval of government support and ensuring fiscal accountability and compliance with the Act.
Allocation of responsibilities in PPP process (including in contract management and regulation)	**PPP Unit** (Department of Finance) to support and act as unit to the committee. The unit replaces the PPP Secretariat established under the PPP Regulations. The unit functions as resource center, coordinating and monitoring and providing advice; is responsible for the process for identification and development of PPPs; analyzes PPPs before submission to Committee; assists procuring authorities administer the Project Facilitation Fund; reviews and advises on requests for government support; liaises with PPP nodes in procuring authorities; and ensures procurement conforms with best practices.
	Procuring Authorities are responsible for development, tender, and implementation of projects.
	PPP Nodes to be established in accordance with the new PPP law in ministries and agencies that are planning to undertake that PPPs are mandates to liaise with the PPP Unit and play a key role on behalf of procuring authorities regarding project development and procurement.
	PPP Committee is responsible for approval of projects (prior to procurement of the project of the feasibility study, prior to negotiation with first-ranked bidder and of negotiated documents after negotiation) (subject relevant to Cabinet approval and/or parliamentary approval), allocation of funds from Project Facilitation Fund. PPP Committee also plays an oversight role of project management by Procuring Authority.
	Debt Management Office carries out fiscal risk assessment of project during project feasibility and after negotiation stage but prior to signature, as well as annual monitoring.
	Cabinet approval (or other entity as delegated by Cabinet)—of full business case of projects.
	Parliamentary approval is needed for concessions for natural resources (cl.71(1) of Constitution).
	Attorney General is responsible for clearance of PPP agreement.

table continues next page

Policy, legal, and regulatory framework

Project selection and procurement

Criteria for selecting potential PPP projects	Procuring entities are responsible for conceptualization and identification. Project appraisal committee to be formed by Procuring Authority which may include one or more members of the relevant PPP Node. Appraisal study needs to demonstrate: comparative advantage for implementation as a PPP; that it is affordable and minimizes as much as possible government support; and that it is commercially viable and attractive to investors and transfers appropriate risk.
Project preparation process and decision making leading to procurement	Procuring Authority to prepare investment appraisal with technical, environmental, social, economic, legal, and financial feasibility under guidance of PPP Unit. PPP Unit can require Procuring Authority to hire transaction advisor.
Treatment of fiscal costs/risks	PPP bill provides that one of functions of PPP Committee will be to ensure fiscal accountability and approval of any and all government support which is extended to PPP projects. Further work is under way to more accurately delineate the role of different parties. This will be detailed either in the regulations of guidelines issued under the authority of the Cabinet Secretary. This will need to be done in light of the roles and responsibilities now set out under the Public Financial Management Bill.

Procurement

Allocation of responsibilities	Procuring Authority responsible for carrying out the tender process.
	PPP Unit oversees procurement process and PPP Committee provides overall monitoring and evaluation.
	Approval required by PPP Committee prior to procurement, negotiation, and then of negotiated agreement. Then goes to Cabinet (unless approval delegated to PPP Committee).
	Debt Management Office carries out fiscal risk assessment.
	Appeals regarding procurement are directed to PPP Committee.
Procurement approaches allowed	Prequalification and competitive tender. Process to be fair, equitable, transparent, competitive, and cost effective.
	Meetings with qualified bidders to discuss specifications prior to issue of invitation to bid permitted.
	Competitive dialogue permitted with each bidder (procuring authority with PPP Unit).
	Points score evaluation system permitted. Bid security can be required. Technical offer and financial offer (technical offer will include input on service levels and specifications). More details to be included in Regulations.
	Committee to then approve entry into negotiations by Proposal Evaluation team with preferred bidder (not to impact nonnegotiable conditions and no amendments to technical and financial terms resulting in a reduction of terms in bid).

table continues next page

Building Integrated Markets within the East African Community
http://dx.doi.org/10.1596/978-1-4648-0227-0

Policy, legal, and regulatory framework	
Unsolicited projects and/or direct negotiation	PPPs (including unsolicited proposals) may be considered for procurement by negotiation without being subject to competitive procurement in exceptional circumstances—urgency, impracticality, unique source or if only one bidder, although one of the exceptions is quite broad referring to "innovative and related intellectual property." Must seek to find alternative methods of procurement before proceeding and must satisfy criteria of value for money, affordability, and risk transfer and **must not** involve any government. A competitive challenge is not required.
Funding/financing of PPPs	
Government resources for PPPs	Project Facilitation Fund described in the PPP Bill—support tender and appraisal, extend viability gap finance, source of liquidity for contingent liabilities. Sources of funds—government grants, development partners, levy from tariffs, aid, and donations.

Source: World Bank.

Tanzania

Policy, legal, and regulatory framework	
PPP policies	National PPP policy issued November 2009 by the Prime Minister's Office (PMO). Defines sectors (all infrastructure, health, education, as well as other sectors). Emphasizes need for transparent/competitive procurement, ensuring proper due diligence including feasibility and appropriate risk allocation.
	PPPs described in introduction to policy as "an arrangement between public and private sector…whereby private entities renovate, construct, operate, maintain and/or manage a facility in accordance with output specifications." Policy mentions management contracts, leases, and concessions for brownfield and a variety of contract structures for greenfield (including DB—design/build).
PPP legislation	**PPP Regulations 2011**—Sets out in detail the PPP process and regulations surrounding project selection, development, and bidding. The PPP Act calls for PPP Finance Regulations to be issued by the Ministry of Finance (MoF) to address, inter alia, unsolicited bids. These are in early draft form and are to be sent to the Cabinet for approval in early summer 2013.
	PPP Act 2010 established the general overall framework for PPPs. Includes creation of two units, PPP Coordination Unit located in Tanzanian Investment Centre (TIC) which reports to the PMO and PPP Finance Unit located in the Ministry of Finance (MoF) and deals with fiscal risk allocation and other financial matters of all PPPs. The only definition of a PPP in the act seems to be "projects undertaken in partnership between the public and private sectors."
	Public Procurement Act 2011 governs procurement of PPPs to the extent not addressed in the PPP Act. Implementing Regulations for this new act have been approved by the Cabinet, and are currently under review by the AG's office.
	Energy and Water Utilities Regulatory Authority Act 2001 established EWURA. **Electricity Act (2008)** and **Water Supply and Sanitation Act 2009** define powers of EWURA in these sectors.

table continues next page

Policy, legal, and regulatory framework	
Implementing regulations	The PPP Regulations 2011 set out the regulations for both the TIC and MoF PPP Unit. Regulations to be issued by MoF (which will address how unsolicited bids are to be managed, inter alia) are currently being developed (intended to be issued mid-2013).
	Implementing Regulations for the Public Procurement (Goods, Works, Non-Consultant Services, and Disposal of Public Assets By Tender) Act 2011 are with the AG's office for comment.
Contracts—standard terms and so on	PPP Act specifies the main areas to be covered in the PPP "agreement."
Institutional structure	
Political/strategic leadership	PMO is one of the main drivers behind the development of the PPP Agenda and sees itself in a coordination role between ministries, departments, and agencies (MDAs), TIC, and MoF PPP units.
Allocation of responsibilities in PPP process (including in contract management and regulation)	**MDAs** (line agencies) have typical set of responsibilities to identify, appraise, develop, and monitor a project to be implemented under this act; they undertake due diligence and submit this to PPP units; they then prepare the request for proposal and run the procurement process. PPP coordinators have been appointed to key line ministries, and PPP Nodes in some (in particular Tanesco, Ministry of Energy and Minerals, Ministry of Transport, and Ministry of Health).
	PPP Coordination Unit has a combination of regulatory and promotional roles, specified in the act as follows: (a) recommends to PPP Finance Unit whether the project: (i) is affordable to the contracting authority; (ii) provides value for money (VfM); (iii) has appropriate risk transfer; (b) ensures feasibility study is properly done; (c) coordinates all PPP projects; (d) advises the government on administrative procedures, and the contracting authority on all matters relating to PPPs; (e) develops guidelines in relation to all matters relating to PPPs; and (f) develops and promotes PPP awareness.
	PPP Finance Unit is located in MoF and has a more closely defined role as dealing with fiscal risk allocation and other financial matters of all PPPs. The unit reviews this and forwards to minister for clearance and allocation of funds.
	PPRA regulates the procurement by government agencies of goods and services. PPP falls under a different regime, but it would appear that the PPRA will regulate procurement rules linked with this regime.
	AG's Office approves legal undertaking of the government.
	EWURA has specific roles in power and water defined by the sector acts: in power, to award licenses (includes generation), fix prices for sale between licensees and to final consumers, approve initiation of procurement and approve license terms and conditions; and, in water, licensing functions, approve tariffs.
	SUMATRA has a role in regulating the marine and surface transport, though it has not been much involved in PPP discussions.
	During implementation—the line agency is responsible for monitoring. PPP Coordination and PPP Finance Units must approve contract amendments.

table continues next page

Policy, legal, and regulatory framework

Project selection and procurement

Criteria for selecting potential PPP projects	The PPP regulations 2011 set out project selection and procurement procedures. PPP Act mentions feasibility studies need to demonstrate comparative advantage in terms of strategic/operational benefits for implementation under the agreement and also criteria relating to risk transfer, VfM, and affordability.
Project preparation process and decision making leading to procurement	Line agency has feasibility study prepared and submits to Coordination Unit which reviews and then forwards to Finance Unit. The law does not seem to mention clearances at earlier stages. If the MoF approves they then proceed with the procurement process. PPP Act specifies the main areas to be covered under the feasibility study, including risk transfer, VfM, and affordability, as well as contract management arrangements. Sector regulators are to be consulted on feasibility studies.
Treatment of fiscal costs/risks	Explicitly mentioned in the role of PPP Finance Unit, although definition of contingent liability is limited. Government reports explicit guarantees such as guaranteed state-owned enterprise (SOE) borrowings.

Procurement

Allocation of responsibilities	MoF approves RFP (where the PPP involves public finance) and MDA can start procurement. Contracting authority initiates process by appointing project officer with appropriate clearance.
	Contracting authority signs following clearance from the Minister of Finance and AG.
	Procurement authority may have a monitoring role as the procurement act will apply to PPPs.
Procurement approaches allowed	A New Public Procurement Act passed by Parliament at the end of 2011 repealed and re-enacted PPA of 2004 and established the Public Procurement Policy Division within the MoF to advise on policy. The Public Procurement Regulatory Authority is maintained, (http://ppra.go.tz/attachments/Act/Public_Procurement_Act_2011.pdf), with a specific part (Part VII) devoted to PPPs. Most of the detail is to be provided in regulations, which are under development. It relates to both solicited and unsolicited proposals and requires projects to get relevant approvals under the PPP Act prior to procurement (section 79). Unsolicited proposals will be subject to formal competitive process as provided in regulations to the PPA (section 80(1)) (yet to be issued at time of report writing) and intellectual property rights of proponents may be acknowledged. Express provision for procurement of transaction advisors (81). Section 72 also specifies that "The tender documents shall specify factors, in addition to price, which may be taken into account in evaluating a tender and how such factors may be quantified or otherwise evaluated."
Unsolicited projects and/or direct negotiation	PPP Act (art. 16) allows for unsolicited projects. The private sector is to present a feasibility study that inter alia explains the financial capacity and ability of the private party in the implementation and management of the proposed project.

table continues next page

Policy, legal, and regulatory framework	
Funding/financing of PPPs	
Government resources for PPPs	No cross-sector subsidy funds (although the MoF refers to a PPP facilitation Fund, much like Kenya's, in its action plan, which is clearly linked to the Project Development Fund mentioned in the PPP Act). The 2009 act on water/sanitation establishes a National Water Investment Fund. There is also a Road Fund that focuses on road repair and maintenance.

Source: World Bank.

Rwanda

Policy, legal, and regulatory framework	
PPP policies	Included in National Public Investment Policy 2009—Government intends to amend in line with draft PPP law[a] and to reflect the institutional and legal framework proposed to be established under the draft PPP law.
	Vision 2020 for Rwanda and Economic Development and Poverty Reduction Strategy Paper—this envisages Rwanda Development Board as playing a key role in private investment promotion, including PPPs.
PPP legislation	The draft Law Governing Public Private Partnerships (2011) (PPP Bill) is proposed to go to Parliament in 2012. It is understood that PPP Bill is currently being redrafted.
	Broad definition of PPP covers management of contracts through to concessions. The draft law currently covers a broad range of sectors including oil and gas and covers traditional infrastructure sectors and social sectors such as health, education, and tourism.
Implementing regulations	PPP regulations and guidelines were scheduled to be developed in 2012. Draft regulations have been prepared and are under consideration by the government.
Contracts—standard terms, and so on	Sections 46 to 69 of PPP Bill set out minimum contractual obligations that PPP agreements will be required to include. The Inter-Ministerial PPP Steering Committee (IPSC) is responsible for approving standards for PPP projects and project documents but team understands that there are no immediate plans to develop standardized documents.
Institutional structure	
Political/strategic leadership	The **Inter-Ministerial PPP Steering Committee (IPSC)** was established under the PPP Act comprising standing members of Minister of National Development Planning, Minister in charge of Finance, Rwanda Development Board (RDB) CEO, together with ex-officio members from ministries with specific projects.
	IPSC shall provide leadership in development of PPP policies and programs and make recommendations to government for its consideration and adoption (12.1).

table continues next page

	Responsible for management of PPP program, development of PPP policies, and implementation of regulations and standards for PPP projects, approval of PPP projects, identification of contracting authority for specific projects, acting as contracting authority for specific projects, approval of Government Financial Support, oversight and review of performance compliance and project execution, review and approval of amendments, maintenance of national asset registry, and making decisions relating to use of funds deriving from PPP appropriations.
Allocation of responsibilities in PPP process (including in contract management and regulation)	**PPP Unit** (currently anticipated to be located in RDB) to assist IPSC and public authorities in all activities relating to PPPs. Functions are to: provide technical assistance and support to contracting authorities and IPSC; make recommendations regarding framework; develop and promulgate procedures and standardized best practices; review and issue opinions regarding viability of proposed projects; make recommendations to IPSC and contracting authorities; scrutinize project proposals, tenders, contracts; monitor and issue opinions regarding level of compliance of contracting authority and private partners; and issue technical opinions.
	Contracting authorities are responsible for proposal, preparation, submission for approval by IPSC and PPP Unit, and implementation of projects.
	IPSC is responsible for approval of projects prior to tender (review of feasibility study) and approval of government financial support. PPP Committee also to play an oversight role of project implementation by procuring authority and private partner. PPP Unit supports IPSC in these roles.
	Other approvals (for example, Cabinet, Parliamentary, Ministry of Finance)—to be determined if IPSC and PPP Unit can charge fees that can be added to PPP transaction (17.2).
Project selection and procurement	
Criteria for selecting potential PPP projects	Details to be in regulations. Contracting authority responsible for conceptualization and identification. Investment grade feasibility study based on VfM as well as sector strategic objectives, technical and commercial feasibility, and ability of project to attract potential private partners and private financing (18.2).
Project preparation process and decision making leading to procurement	Contracting authority to prepare investment grade project feasibility study (18).
	Submitted to PPP Unit and IPSC for review and approval (with exception of small local projects).
Treatment of fiscal costs/risks	The draft PPP Bill does not address contingent liabilities.
Procurement	
Allocation of responsibilities	Procuring Authority responsible for carrying out the tender process and Rwanda Public Procurement Authority (RPPA) oversees procurement process. A number of provisions of Law on Public Procurement (Law 63 of 2007) including appeal process and enforcement powers of RPPA which may need to be clarified with respect to the draft PPP law. Approval required by ISPC prior to tender and publication of notification of award is required (43).

table continues next page

Policy, legal, and regulatory framework	
Procurement approaches allowed	As per draft PPP bill, prequalification and competitive tender. Shortlisting of bidders possible.
	One- or two-stage bidding—in case of two-stage bidding, meetings with qualified bidders to discuss specifications prior to issue of final invitation to bid permitted. Points score evaluation system permitted. Bid security can be required. Technical offer and financial offer but not clear whether they are to be in separate envelopes.
	Contracting authority may enter into negotiations with bidder that has attained best ranking, provided that negotiations do not impinge on contractual terms defined as nonnegotiable in the final request for proposals that were issued by the government.
Unsolicited projects and/or direct negotiation	Unsolicited proposals may be considered by contracting authorities as long as they do not relate to a project for which selection procedures have been initiated or announced (39). If project potentially in public interest, contracting authority can invite proponent to give detailed information—contracting authority can then carry out proper evaluation. If contracting authority wants to proceed, shall submit to IPSC for authorization. If authorization given, full competitive tender required (proponent shall be invited to participate in competitive selection procedure with no advantage mentioned in law). In exceptional circumstances, projects can proceed to direct negotiation (36).
Funding/financing of PPPs	
Government resources for PPPs	PPP bill contemplates different types of government support as possibilities. As noted above, one of the functions of the IPSC is to approve government financial support for projects, although specifics on how this would be done, or the role of the Ministry of Finance, are not yet available.

Source: World Bank.
a. There is a draft PPP law shared with World Bank as of May 30, 2011 and the summary reflects the provisions of that draft.

Uganda

Policy, legal, and regulatory framework	
PPP policies	PPP Framework Policy was issued in March 2010 by Ministry of Finance (MoF). Defines sectors (all infrastructure, health, education, as well as other sectors). Includes statement of principles (VfM, public interest, risk allocation, output oriented, transparency, accountability, and competitive tender). Covers project development; stakeholder consultations; public awareness; roles and responsibilities; monitoring and evaluation process; and audit processes.
PPP legislation	PPP Bill is drafted and will be released for public comments.
	Public Procurement and Disposal of Public Assets (PPDA) Act 2003 governs procurement of PPPs and has a specific section on PPPs (Section 243.1–243.4). Other laws which have relevance to PPPs include Public Finance and Accountability Act 2003, National Audit Act 2008, Local Government Act 1997, and Contract Laws of 1963, 2008.
	Sector legislations relevant to PPPs are Electricity Act 1999, Water Act 1995, and National Water Policy 1999.

table continues next page

Policy, legal, and regulatory framework	
Implementing regulations	PPP Bill currently being developed will also entail preparation of regulations. Public Procurement and Disposal of Public Assets (PPDA) Act 2003 also has regulations.
Contracts	PPP Framework Policy mentions that standardized contract will be used.
Institutional structure	
Political/strategic leadership	President and MoF are leading the PPP agenda. There is no cross-sector forum for PPPs yet.
Allocation of responsibilities in PPP process (including in contract management and regulation)	The following is stated in the PPP Framework Policy. However, there are some gray areas, including when Cabinet approval is required, and when and for which projects the PPP Unit will provide assistance to contracting agencies.
	MoF is responsible for providing funding and oversight for the PPP Unit; developing policies and guidelines for implementing PPPs; advising government on the financial implications of any PPP project; quality assurance on the economic appraisal and VfM; and taking into consideration the financial obligations imposed on the national budget.
	Cabinet will give approval for all PPP projects when feasibility study report is submitted and before contract award.
	Contracting agencies have typical set of responsibilities to identify, develop, and manage PPP projects.
	PPP Unit is responsible for advising on the appropriate use of PPPs in the National Development Plan; providing guidance and support to government institutions; promoting a consistent approach to PPP project development; and disseminating best practice guidance. (General observation within the country is that privatization unit within the MoF will be the responsible unit for the PPP agenda, but this is not confirmed in any public document yet.)
	The PPDA Authority may issue guideline for PPPs and can be consulted on contractual forms which are not specified in the PPDA Act. However, it is not clear to what extent these rules are being applied.
	For energy sector, Electricity Regulatory Authority (ERA) must issue licenses to any new provider.
	Water supply services in 19 large urban towns are the mandate of the National Water and Sewerage Corporation (NWSC), a commercialized, publicly owned utility established in 1972. NWSC currently also owns and manages the assets of 18 of the 44 largest towns in Uganda. Directorate of Water Development must issue permit to any entity involved in water use, and most municipality governments have established their own water authorities.
Project selection and procurement	
Criteria for selecting potential PPP projects	This may be included in the PPP Bill but presumably will be developed in the regulations/guidelines. PPP Framework Policy states that feasibility study reports should be submitted to MoF and the Cabinet for approval before any projects can be further developed.
Project preparation process and decision making leading to procurement	Feasibility study phase—For all PPP projects, contracting agency prepares feasibility study and submits to MoF and the Cabinet for approval.

table continues next page

Policy, legal, and regulatory framework

	Project delivery phase-project team is appointed which will develop a project plan, and tender documents; "Expressions of Interest" (EOI); an RFP; a negotiation team will negotiate with the preferred bidder; MoF approves contract terms including financial close, monitoring for project delivery and service outputs, and public communication and awareness.
Treatment of fiscal costs/risks	MoF is responsible for advising government on PPP project fiscal implications. There is no explicit mention of contingent liability. Unclear if government provides explicit guarantees other than PPA.
Procurement	
Allocation of responsibilities	Contracting authority and a project team (composed of project officer, experts, and steering committee) are mainly responsible for procuring projects.
Procurement approaches allowed	PPP procurement requires a tendering process based on the principles of transparency, competitiveness, and fairness. Competitive dialogue can be used to obtain value for money for the project. The overall procurement procedure is EOI->shortlisting->RFP->selection of preferred bidder->negotiation->approval from MoF->contract award
Unsolicited projects and/or direct negotiation	Unsolicited project proposals are allowed and are subject to a competitive tendering process. The proponent may be compensated for proprietary interest or costs in accordance with guidelines that will be issued for the treatment of unsolicited proposals.
Funding/Financing of PPPs	
Government resources for PPPs	No specialized funds for PPPs at present.

Source: World Bank.

Building Integrated Markets within the East African Community
http://dx.doi.org/10.1596/978-1-4648-0227-0

PPP Portfolios in EAC Partner States

http://dx.doi.org/10.1596/978-1-4648-0227-0

Project name	Sector	Estimated cost (US$ million)	Status	PPP type	Source[a]	Notes
Burundi						
Telecoms						
Telecel Burundi	Mobile access	15.5	Financial Close 06/1993. Operational. 22 year.	Merchant	PPI database	
Spacetel Burundi	Mobile access	16	Financial Close 01/2000. Operational. 15 year.	Merchant	PPI database	
Africell	Mobile access	22	Financial Close 01/2000. Operational. 15 year.	Merchant	PPI database	
Tanzania						
Power						
Tanwat Wood-Fired Power Plant	Generation	6	Financial Close 01/1994. Concluded. 6 year.	Build, lease, and transfer	PPI database	2.5 MW
Independent Power Tanzania Ltd	Generation	127	Financial Close 06/1997. Operational. 20 year.	Build, operate, transfer (BOT)	PPI database	100 MW
Songas—Songo Songo Gas to Power Project	Generation, Natural Gas transmission	316	Financial Close 11/2001. Operational. 20 year.	BOT	PPI database	Supported by IDA project (P002797), capacity at present 305 MW
Tanzania Electricity Supply Company (TANESCO)	Generation, distribution, and transmission		Financial Close 12/2002. Concluded. 4 year.	Management contract	PPI database	Contract second phase not extended, reversion to state management.[b]
Mtwara Region Gas-to-Power Project	Generation	32	Financial Close 06/2005. Operational. 25 year.	Build, own, operate (BOO)	PPI database	12 MW
Aggreko Ubungo Temporary Power Station	Generation	6.31	Financial Close 10/2006. Operational. 5 year.	Rental	PPI database	50 MW, the contract with Agrekko for temporary power provision was extended
Dowans Lease Power Ubungo	Generation	15.78	Financial Close 06/2006. Concluded. 2 year.	Rental	PPI database	100 MW
Alstom Power Rentals Mwanza	Generation	6.31	Financial Close 09/2006. Operational.	Rental	PPI database	40 MW

table continues next page

Project name	Sector	Estimated cost (US$ million)	Status	PPP type	Source[a]	Notes
Aggreko Ubungo and Tegeta Temporary Power Station	Generation		Financial Close 07/2011. Operational.	Rental	PPI database	
Symbion Dodoma Power Plant	Generation	4.7	Financial Close 11/2011. Operational.	Rental	PPI database	
Symbion Rental Ubungo Power Plant	Generation	129.4	Financial Close 5/2011. Operational.	Rental	PPI database	
Transport						
Kilimanjaro International Airport	Airport	11.5	Financial Close 11/1998. Canceled. 25 year.	Rehabilitate, operate, transfer	PPI database	
Kidatu Transhipment Facility	Railroad	5	Financial Close 06/1998. Operational. 20 year.	BOT	PPI database	
Dar es Salaam Container Terminal	Port	6.5	Financial Close 01/2000. Operational. 10 year, extended to 25 years in 2005.	Rehabilitate, operate, transfer	PPI database	Very successful up to 2005. Dwell times have increased after concession extension.[c]
Tanzanian Railways	Railroad	111	Financial Close 09/2007. 25 year. TRL renationalized in 2010.	Rehabilitate, operate, transfer	PPI database	Rail traffic overestimated, partly due to improved roads. Govt increased salaries. Increased fuel levy.[d]
Air Tanzania Company Limited	Airline		Financial Close 2002. Renationalized 12/2006.	Divestiture, partial (51 percent)	Adam Nelsson, World Bank.	Continues to requireUS$0.5m subsidy/month and does[e]
Water and Sanitation						
Dar es Salaam Water Distribution	Water utility with sewerage	8.5	Financial Close 02/2003. Canceled. 10 year terminated 2005.	Lease contract	PPI database	Reasons for failure: The winning consortium lacked experience running a large water utility. Inability to collect revenue, water losses, and unable to persuade regulator to increase tariffs.[f]

table continues next page

Project name	Sector	Estimated cost (US$ million)	Status	PPP type	Source[a]	Notes
Telecoms						
Mobitel Tanzania	Fixed and mobile access	645.2	Financial Close 06/1993. Operational.	BOO	PPI database	
Tritel Telecommunications	Mobile access	24.6	Financial Close 06/1995. Canceled. 15 year.	Merchant	PPI database	
Jupiter Communications	Fixed access	0.2	Financial Close 06/1996. Concluded. 15 year but termination year is 2005.	BOO	PPI database	
Adesemi Tanzania Ltd.	Fixed access	8	Financial Close 06/1996. Merged. 15 year contract terminated in 1999.	BOO	PPI database	
Zanzibar Telecom Limited	Mobile access	495	Financial Close 01/1997. 15 year.	Merchant	PPI database	
Vodacom Tanzania	Mobile access	871.9	Financial Close 12/1999. Operational. 15 year.	Merchant	PPI database	
Tanzanian Telecommunications Company Limited	Mobile, fixed, long distance	94.5	Financial Close 03/2001. 2005 split into TTCL (fixed, reverted to govt) and Celtel (mobile, privately owned)	Divestiture, partial	PPI database	
Airtel Tanzania	Mobile access	616	Financial Close 08/2005. Operational.	Merchant	PPI database	
Kenya						
Power						
Iberafrica Power Ltd.	Generation	64	Financial Close 8/1996. Concluded. 15 year.	BOT	PPI database	56 MW
Mombasa Barge-Mounted Power Project	Generation	35	Financial Close 1/1996. Concluded. 7 year.	BOO	PPI database	46 MW

table continues next page

Project name	Sector	Estimated cost (US$ million)	Status	PPP type	Source[a]	Notes
Kipevu II	Generation	85	Financial Close 09/1999. Operational. 20 year.	BOO	PPI database	75 MW
Ormat Olkaria III Geothermal Power plant (phase 1 and 2)	Generation	159	Financial Close 01/1999. Operational. 20 year.	BOO	PPI database	61 MW. World Bank support loan
Kenya Electricity Generating Company Limited	Generation		Financial Close 05/2006. Operational.	Divestiture, partial	PPI database	945 MW. 30 %sold, 70 %state owned
Kenya Power and Lighting Company Management Contract	Distribution and transmission		Financial Close 05/2006. Concluded. 2 year.	Management contract	PPI database	Successful: 800,000 connections, increased revenues, the only energy distributor in region operating without state subsidy.[9]
Aggreko Embakassi and Eldoret Power Stations	Generation	7.89	Financial Close 04/2006. Operational. 5 year.	Rental	PPI database	100 MW
Rabai Power Plant	Generation	155	Financial Close 10/2008. Construction. 20 year.	BOT	PPI database	90 MW
Mumias Power Plant	Generation	50	Financial Close 07/2008. Operational.	BOO	PPI database	35 MW
Aggreko 140 MW temporary rental power plant	Generation	11	Financial Close 09/2009. Concluded. 2 year.	Rental	PPI database	140 MW
Aggreko Western Kenya Temporary Power Station	Generation	4.7	Financial Close 07/2011. Operational.	Rental	PPI database	
Transport						
Mombasa Container Terminal	Port	0	Financial Close 08/1996. Canceled. 2 year.	Management contract	PPI database	
Mombasa Grain Terminal	Port	32	Financial Close 04/1998. Operational.	BOO	PPI database	Well functioning.
Jomo Kenyatta Airport Cargo Terminal	Airport	21.4	Financial Close 5/1998. Operational. 40 year.	BOT	PPI database	JKIA cargo handling is currently managed by 4 different contractors on the BOT basis.[h]

table continues next page

Project name	Sector	Estimated cost (US$ million)	Status	PPP type	Source[a]	Notes
Kenya-Uganda Railways	Railroad	250	Financial Close 12/2006. Restructured in 2011. 25 year.	Rehabilitate, operate, and transfer	PPI database	Joint Uganda-Kenya project. The first contractor didn't bring necessary investment which caused deterioration. Social safeguards triggered: resettlement of population along the rail line.[i]
Water and Sanitation						
Malindi water utility contract	Water utility with sewerage		Financial close 01/1999. Concluded. 5 year.	Management contract	PPI database	
Telecoms						
Safaricom	Mobile access	2027	Financial Close 12/1999. Operational. 15 year.	Merchant	PPI database	
Airtel Kenya	Mobile access	1512.8	Financial Close 11/1999. Operational. 15 year.	Merchant	PPI database	
Econet Kenya Limited	Mobile access	75	Financial Close 12/2004. Operational. 15 year.	Merchant	PPI database	
Telkom Kenya	Fixed, mobile access, and long distance	76	Financial Close 12/2007. Operational.	Divestiture, partial	PPI database	49% noncontrolling share kept by govt. Registering losses and may go bankrupt in 5 years.[j]
TEAMS[k]	Submarine cable					
SEACOM	Submarine cable					
Uganda						
Power						
Kasese Electrification Project	Distribution and transmission		Financial Close 11/2003. Operational.	Rehabilitate, operate, transfer	PPI database	Supplied electricity to population of 53,000.
Western Nile Electrification Project	Generation, distribution, and transmission	11.3	Financial Close 03/2003. Operational. 20 year.	Rehabilitate, operate, transfer	PPI database	3.5 MW

table continues next page

Project name	Sector	Estimated cost (US$ million)	Status	PPP type	Source[a]	Notes
Uganda Electricity Generation Company Limited	Generation	6.8	Financial Close 04/2003. Operational. 20 year.	Rehabilitate, lease or rent, transfer	PPI database	300 MW Run by Eskom, relatively successful.
Umeme Limited	Distribution	65	Financial Close 03/2005. Operational. 20 year.	Rehabilitate, lease or rent, transfer	PPI database	838,000 connections. Run by Actis, concession to be re-evaluated by the government at the end of 2012.[l]
Aggreko Kampala Temporary Power Station	Generation	11.83	Financial Close 04/2005. Operational. 6 year.	Rental	PPI database	50 MW. Raised environmental concerns being near a residential area.
Aggreko Jinja Temporary Power Station	Generation	11.8	Financial Close 04/2006. Operational. 5 year.	Rental	PPI database	50 MW
Kakira cogeneration plant	Generation	43	Financial Close 10/2006. Operational.	Build, own, operate	PPI database	
Bujagali Hydro Project	Generation	799[m]	Financial Close 12/2007. Construction. 30 year.	BOT	PPI database	250 MW. Delayed by environmental issues, should have been operational in 2004. First potential investor, AES, backed out of the deal.
Aggreko Mutundwe thermal plant project	Generation	11.8	Financial Close 08/2007. Concluded. 3 year.	Rental	PPI database	50 MW. Plant was closed at the end of 2011 after an accident.
ECO Ishasha Mini Hydropower Plant	Generation	14	Financial Close 06/2008. Operational.	Build, operate, and transfer	PPI database	
Kinyara Cogeneration Plant	Generation		Financial Close 01/2009. Operational.	Build, own, operate	PPI database	
Tororo Power Station	Generation	32	Financial Close 12/2009. Operational.	Build, own, operate	PPI database	
Bugoye Hydro Electric Power Project	Generation	35	Financial Close 11/2008. Construction. 30 year.	BOT	PPI database	13 MW
Mpanga Hydro Power Project	Generation	23	Financial Close 11/2008. Operational. 20 year.	BOT	PPI database	18 MW

table continues next page

Project name	Sector	Estimated cost (US$ million)	Status	PPP type	Source[a]	Notes
Namanve Power Plant	Generation	93	Financial Close 09/2008. Operational. 6 year.	BOT	PPI database	50 MW
Buseruka Hydropower Plant	Generation	27	Financial Close 05/2009. Construction. 30 year.	BOT	PPI database	9 MW
Uganda Small Scale Power	Generation				WB supported PPPs	IFC Advisory supported.
Transport						
Kenya-Uganda Railways	Railroad	250	Financial Close 12/2006. Restructured in 2011. 25 year.	Rehabilitate, operate, and transfer	PPI database	Joint Uganda-Kenya. The first contractor didn't bring necessary investment which caused deterioration. Social safeguards triggered: resettlement of population along the rail line.
Water And Sanitation						
Kampala Revenue Improvement Project	Water utility with sewerage	0	Financial Close 01/1998. Concluded. 3 year.	Management contract	PPI database	Very limited success. Expensive and poor incentive framework.
ONDEO Services Uganda Limited	Water utility with sewerage	0	Financial Close 01/2002. Concluded. 2 year.	Management contract	PPI database	Very limited success. Expensive and poor incentive framework.
Uganda Rural Water	Water utility with sewerage				WB supported PPPs	IFC Advisory supported.
Telecoms						
Airtel Uganda	Mobile access	372.1	Financial Close 06/1994. Operational.	Merchant	PPI database	
MTN Uganda	Mobile and fixed access	826.1	Financial Close 06/1998. Operational. 15 year.	BOO	PPI database	

table continues next page

Project name	Sector	Estimated cost (US$ million)	Status	PPP type	Source[a]	Notes
Uganda Telecommunications Limited	Mobile, fixed, and long distance	264	Financial Close 02/1999. Operational.	Divestiture, partial	PPI database	
Warid Telecom Uganda Limited	Mobile, fixed, and long distance	681	Financial Close 12/2007. Operational.	Merchant	PPI database	
Orange Uganda	Mobile access	34	Financial Close 10/2008. Operational.	Merchant	PPI database	
Rwanda						
Power						
Electrogaz	Distribution, transmission, and generation		Financial Close 06/2003. Canceled 2006. 5 year.	Management contract	PPI database	92,000 connections.
Aggreko 10 MW Power Station Rwanda	Generation	1.58	Financial Close 09/2005. Operational. 6 year.	Rental	PPI database	10 MW
Kibuye Power 1	Generation	76	Financial Close 03/2005. Cancelled.	Build, own, and operate	PPI database	
InfraV-LakeKivu	Generation	4			WB supported PPPs	IFC
KivuWatt	Generation	142			WB supported PPPs	MIGA
Water and Sanitation						
Rwanda Urban Water	Water/Sanitation				WB supported PPPs	IFC Advisory supported.
Telecoms						
MTN Rwanda	Mobile access	226.5	Financial Close 06/1998. Operational.	Merchant	PPI database	

table continues next page

Project name	Sector	Estimated cost (US$ million)	Status	PPP type	Source[a]	Notes
Rwandatel - First Divestiture	Mobile, fixed, long distance		Financial Close 11/2005. Canceled 2007.	Divestiture, partial	PPI database	
Rwandatel - Second Divestiture	Mobile, fixed, long distance		Financial Close 10/2007. Operational.	Divestiture, partial	PPI database	
Millicom Rwanda	Mobile access	61	Financial Close 01/2009. Operational. 15 year.	Merchant	PPI database	

Source: This includes data from the PPI Database as well as additional projects provided by contacts with Member States' PPP Units.

a. PPI database found at http://www.ppiaf.org
b. Nelsson 2011.
c. Ibid.
d. Ibid.
e. Ibid.
f. Ibid.
g. Interview with Eng. Stanley Kamau, Director of PPP Unit, Kenya.
h. Ibid.
i. Interview with Eng. Stanley Kamau, Director of PPP Unit, Kenya, and David Ssebabi and Otweyo Orono, Privatisation Unit, Uganda.
j. Ibid.
k. Ibid.
l. Interview with David Ssebabi and Otweyo Orono, Privatisation Unit, Uganda.
m. Ibid.

Rift Valley Railway Case

Introduction

The Kenya-Uganda Railway is a major regional railway line in East Africa, extending from the port of Mombasa on the east coast of Kenya to Malaba southeast of the town of Tororo on the border with Uganda (1,083 kilometers) (see map C.1). It connects major towns in Kenya such as Nairobi, Nakuru, and Eldoret, with a main branch line to Kisumu (217 kilometers), a major port on Lake Victoria. The line also runs into Uganda, connecting Tororo, Jinja, and Kampala, the capital of Uganda, with branch lines to the oil producing region near Lake Albert. It is a meter-gauge line built almost 100 years ago (1896–1905) during the colonial era. It was then known as the Lunatic Express because of the harsh environment under which it was built and operated. When it was finally completed, the 2,350 kilometers rail line played a key role in the early development of East Africa by serving for decades as the most important means for moving goods and people between inland population centers and the seaport of Mombasa.

Political Economy Issues

Political problems within the East African Community (EAC) resulted in the balkanization of the then East African Railways and Harbors (EARH), finally leading to the creation of national railways in 1978, following the collapse of

Map C.1 East African Railway System

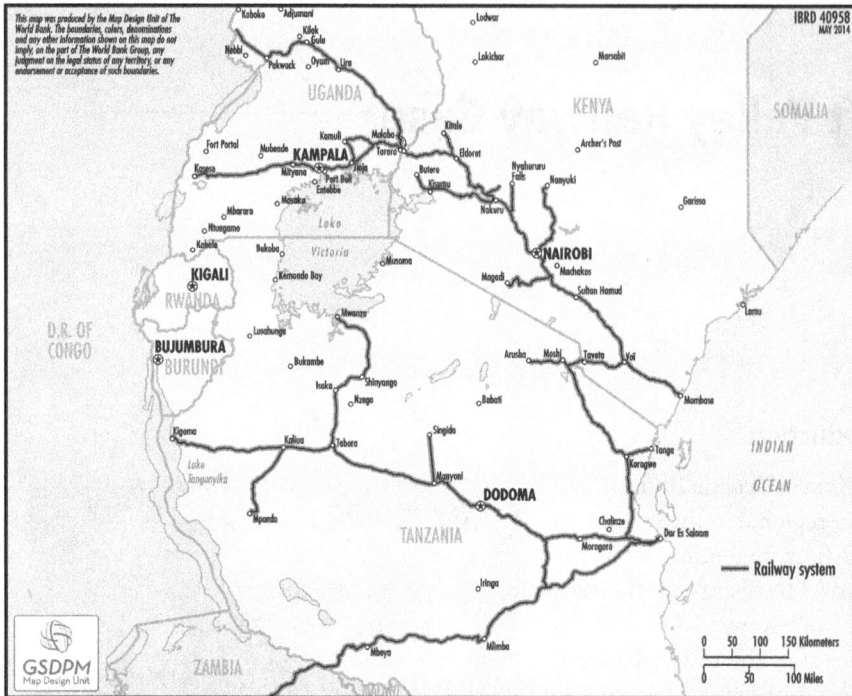

Source: East African Railways Master Plan Study, Final Report, CPCS, January 2009.

the EAC. With respect to the railways, Kenya was left with the prime assets of EARH, such as the main workshops in Nairobi. The civil strife in Uganda and virtual collapse of Uganda Railways Corporation (URC) during the 1970s lost Kenya Railways Corporation (KRC) much of its longest distance and most profitable freight market; average freight haul distance fell by 25 percent. The weaknesses of KRC and URC management within a government-controlled environment became increasingly manifest. Tariffs could not be increased in line with inflation, and asset renewal fell accordingly. Political involvement in the appointment and tenure of senior management increased and salaries and benefits began to fall in real terms. Development partners attempted to assist with the commercialization of the management and operation of the two rail-ways, but there was no strong commitment from the respective governments of the time. The rail business began a steady decade-long slide into insolvency as maintenance and investment lagged, revenues dropped, and the workforce continued to expand.

By 1992, the Kenyan government, responsible for most of this stretch of rail infrastructure, employed 22,000 workers to look after it, an estimated 15,000 more than necessary. In the 2004/05 fiscal year, the annual cargo tonnage slipped to 1.9 million tons, less than 20 percent of total east-west shipping. By

June of 2004, KRC had accumulated US$277 million in debt, with annual losses running at about US$39 million. For average Kenyans and Ugandans, travel anywhere along the line was cheaper by taxi and took half the time. For the manufacturing sector, it was less costly to ship a 20-foot container from Chicago to the port of Mombasa than it was to transport that container via rail from Mombasa to Nairobi.

Background of the Rift Valley Railways

During the 1990s, KRC lost the confidence of its customer base, and the situation shifted from being capacity constrained to being demand constrained, requiring a major effort to bring back traffic to rail. Tariffs were increased to maintain revenues, to such levels that it became cheaper to move containers by road rather than rail. Subsequently, the overall performance of the Kenya-Uganda Railway was affected largely by events in Kenya and its management by KRC. At the height of its performance in the early 1970s, the line carried nearly 4.5 million tons of freight per annum, of which about 25–30 percent was transit traffic, nearly two-thirds of it Uganda bound. However, increased competition from an aggressive road transport sector,[1] and KRC's inability to provide the level of service and capacity demanded led to a drastic decline in the volume of freight carried (see figure C.1), such that by 1997 it had fallen to 1.6 million tons. After a brief increase to 2.2 million tons in 2001, the traffic in 2007 dropped to less than 2 million tons in Kenya and less than 750,000 tons per annum in Uganda (CPCS Transcom International 2009). Although interim data are not available, in 2010, the line carried 1.6 million tons per annum (Uganda less than 300,000 tons) with a revenue base of only US$66 million (95 percent cargo and 5 percent passenger) as opposed to the anticipated US$120 million.

Figure C.1 Kenya Railways Freight Traffic, 1971–2001

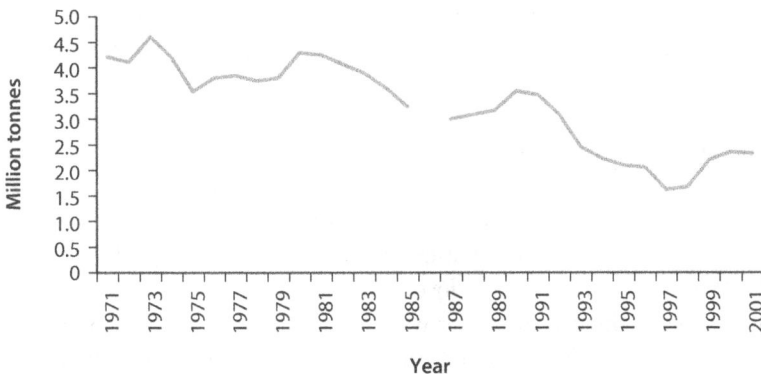

Source: World Bank 2002.

Table C.1 Kenya Railways: Passenger Market, 1971–2001

	1971	1979	1989	1992	1995	1998	1999	2000	2001
No.'000	1,773	1,763	3,700	2,599	1,624	2,849	3,870	4,201	4,120
Pass-km	273	499	823	586	363	347	299	302	289
Av.km	154	283	222	225	224	122	77	72	70

Source: World Bank.

Passenger traffic showed a different pattern, with major changes in the passenger market in the period 1971–2001 (table C.1).

In the 1980s, both passenger numbers and kilometers rose substantially. Thereafter, passenger kilometers fell steadily, but passenger numbers more than doubled after 1995. Long-distance passenger services in the early 2000s were either suspended or their frequency reduced, while short-distance Nairobi commuter traffic expanded. While having social benefits, the commuter service was the largest loss-making activity.

The situation in Uganda was no different, with URC incurring a loss every year, performing little or no maintenance of the infrastructure and rolling stock, and making near zero investments in capital projects. This situation led both governments (Kenya and Uganda) to consider privatizing their respective railways. In 2002, International Finance Corporation (IFC) was commissioned in Kenya and a private sector consultant in Uganda to conduct a feasibility study and develop an appropriate framework for concessioning the two railways in the respective countries.

At the time, there was no appropriate legal and regulatory framework for private sector ownership and operation of railway assets. A World Bank Public-Private Infrastructure Advisory Facility (PPIAF) commissioned study in Kenya looked at various options (Adam Smith Institute 2003). A number of regulatory regimes were examined:

- Modal regulators—a separate regulator for rail, ports, civil aviation, and possibly roads
- Sector regulator —a single regulator to cover the entire transport sector
- Multisector regulator—a regulator to cover the transport sector and some or all of the utility sectors.

Following an extensive debate and numerous stakeholder consultations, the recommendation focused on establishing a sector regulator, excepting aviation (as is the case of SUMATRA[2] in Tanzania), but the recommendation was never implemented. No such regulatory framework was adopted in Uganda either.

By 2003, the two countries were close to inviting bids for concessioning their respective railways to the private sector when, under an agreement signed by the two presidents in July 2003, the governments decided to concession the railway jointly under one ownership and management. In December 2003, the IFC team met with the Government of Kenya (GoK) and the Government of Uganda (GoU) to finalize the joint transaction structure. The meetings resulted in an memorandum of understanding (MoU) drafted by the Joint Steering Committee, which contained provisions on an agreed joint concessioning structure and a work plan. Premarketing meetings with investors in the United States, Canada, the United Kingdom, and South Africa were carried out in June 2004, and stakeholders and local investors conferences were held in Nairobi in July 2004.

The decision to go with one joint concession for the two railways was a good one, considering the need for seamless operation across the border, the need for regional integration, and the extreme interdependence of the two railways. The main objectives of the proposed joint concession were identified as follows:[3]

- Seamless and more efficient operations
- Bigger market share for the long-distance freight
- More efficient utilization of operating assets such as locomotives and wagons (rolling stock) and other assets such as workshops, plants, and equipment
- Availability of a wider range of equipment and facilities to choose from, hence providing the option of using only the best serviceable equipment and facilities
- Reduced cost of operations resulting from longer haulage distance for which railway has a competitive advantage
- Attraction of a greater number of investors
- Stimulation of faster economic growth in the region.

Project Preparation

Management of Project Development
As in all complex Public-Private Partnership (PPP) projects, the development and management of concessioning the Kenya-Uganda Railways required careful planning and execution of all steps, from mobilizing the preparation team to awarding the contract and concluding the transaction. This task was entrusted to the Advisory Services arm of the IFC with an explicit mandate to conduct all the requisite studies, perform due diligence, look at alternative structures for PPP, recommend a specific strategy and framework, gauge the private investor interest, and finally procure a qualified concessionaire and bring the transaction to financial close.

Project Objectives and Design
The objectives behind the privatization of Kenya-Uganda Railway operations were threefold: (i) to mobilize external resources to revamp the grossly deteriorated assets; (ii) to provide seamless and efficient operation of the railway across the two countries and enhance regional integration; and (iii) to recapture a bigger market share of the freight transport business in the region.

The project was designed as a 25-year unitary (vertically integrated) concession wherein the concessionaire would own, maintain, and operate all core assets conceded under the contract and make investments for future expansion. The only exception was for the trains operated by the Magadi Railway Company (MRC) on behalf of the Magadi Soda Company, which was granted a license by the Ministry of Transport to operate over KRC tracks and use rolling stock leased from KRC until the year 2023. Since 1997, the MRC has transported soda ash, other products, and supplies (mainly fuel) between a terminal at Mombasa and the soda ash plant at Magadi, 115 kilometers southwest of Nairobi. With regard to passenger services, the selected concessionaire would be required to operate passenger trains at a designated frequency for five years and thereafter would have the option to continue or allow third-party operations under an open access regime.

Procurement Process

Seven firms, all international consortiums, were prequalified on the basis, inter alia, of the following two key qualification criteria:

1. A net worth of US$35 million or provision of a bank letter confirming availability of a credit line of at least US$35 million
2. Experience with running a railway with annual freight volumes of at least 250 billion net ton kilometers (ntkm) and 300 route kilometers.

Bids were opened in public in September 2005. Only two consortiums submitted their bids: RITES Ltd. (India) with Magadi Soda Company (UK) Consortium and Sheltam Trade Close (South Africa), bidding as Rift Valley Railway Consortium. Following technical evaluation, both bids were found responsive. The financial proposals of both bidders were opened in public in October 2005. Rift Valley Railways (RVR) Consortium won, having offered 11.1 percent of the gross revenue for the concession term, US$1.0 million per annum for passenger services, and an upfront entry fee of US$3.0 million to Kenya and US$2.0 million to Uganda. RITES, on the other hand, offered concession fees of 6.01–6.04 percent and required a subsidy of US$6 million for passenger services.

Structure of the Concession

Concession Agreements. Two separate mirror concession agreements were signed with subsidiary companies of RVR—one with Kenya and another with Uganda. RVR remained the holding company with Sheltham as the Lead Shareholder (35 percent). The others were Transcentury (20 percent), Primefuels (15 percent), Centum (10 percent), Mirambo (10 percent), and Babock and Brown (10 percent). To deal with cross-border issues as well as to provide for a coordinated operation across the two countries, an Interface Agreement was signed by all parties. Furthermore, Direct Agreements were also signed by IFC and Kreditanstalt für Wiederaufbau (Reconstruction Credit Institute; KfW) as the main lenders of the concession.

Conceded Assets Account. A unique and innovative feature of the concession was the establishment of a Conceded Assets Account (CAA). All the railway core assets were conceded by the governments to the concession companies. But these were assets conceded for use, with ownership of the infrastructure still resting with the respective governments. The assets handed over to the concessionaires would be accounted for as concessionaire liabilities to the government and amortized accordingly. Newly acquired or improved assets, such a rolling stock, would be amortized under the same account, but treated as credits to the concessionaires. By auditing the account frequently, the amortization of these investments can be monitored, and the value added to the railway business. This CAA is designed to be the basis on which the accounts between the concessionaire and the governments will be reconciled, whenever the deal is terminated or upon its natural expiration.

Mitigation of Political Risks. Governments' willingness and ability to make good on obligations relating to the CAA were supported by two separate World Bank Partial Risk Guarantees (PRGs). These are guarantees to the respective concession companies—US$45 million for RVR-Kenya and US$15 million for RVR-Uganda. The PRGs would be triggered by the failure of either government to meet its contract termination payment obligations relating to the CAA. These mechanisms (summarized in figure C.2) had never before been structured into a long-term infrastructure concession contract, and seem to have played a key role in the eventual financial closure of this deal (Leigland 2007).

Institutional and Regulatory Framework

Although this was a regional PPP, the EAC played little or no role in the development and conclusion of the concession and there was no regional policy framework to guide such a complex and crucial endeavor. To get around this gap, the Interface Agreement provided for the setting up of a Joint Railway Commission (an advisory body) to facilitate coordination and resolution of cross-border issues. Otherwise, in effect, there were two

Figure C.2 Kenya-Uganda Railway Concession Structure

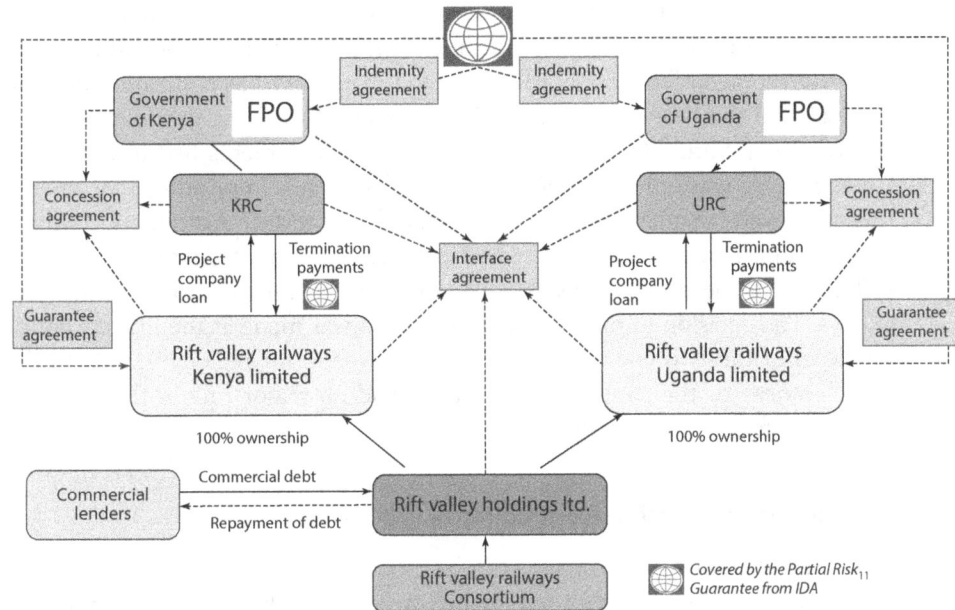

Source: World Bank
Note: KRC = Kenya Railways Corporation; URC = Uganda Railways Corporation.

Building Integrated Markets within the East African Community
http://dx.doi.org/10.1596/978-1-4648-0227-0

Table C.2 Original Project Cost Estimate and Financing Plan

Project cost	Amount ($m)	Project financing	Amount ($m)
Track	33.0	Equity	24.0
Locomotives	20.0	Debt	64.0
Wagons	28.0	Internal Cash Flow	23.0
Other (workshops, equipment, and so on)	10.0		
Total capital expenditures	91.0		
Other uses	20.0		
Total investment	**111.0**	**Total financing**	**111.0**

separate concessions (RVR-Kenya and RVR-Uganda), two separate asset owners (KRC and URC on behalf of the two governments), and an Interface Agreement among all parties concerned to guide resolution of common issues affecting both concessions.

Financing Arrangements

Table C.2 gives a summary of the estimated investment cost (total US$111.0 million) and the financing plan for the concession, with a debt to equity ratio of 2.7:1. About US$23.0 million was expected to be generated internally from profits and reinvested as capital.

Key Regional Aspects of the Joint Concession

Having two key stakeholders at the national level made the project regional in character with implications for other neighboring countries such as Rwanda, Burundi, South Sudan, East Democratic Republic of Congo, and Ethiopia. As a result, the need for cross-border legal and regulatory harmonization became critical, and this was solved only with an interim measure, the Joint Railway Commission. Similarly, two separate concession agreements had to be signed, though there was only one operator, which had major implications for financing and sovereign guarantees and necessitated an Interface Agreement. To mitigate political risks, separate Institutional Development Association (IDA) PRGs had to be brokered, backed by sovereign guarantees from Uganda and Kenya. The decision to make a joint concession was made at the highest political level in the two countries with no clear avenue for regional inputs to the development of the concession. The EAC had no major role in the development and facilitation of the concession.

Saving the Concession from Collapse (2006–10)

Poor Performance

Poor management and weak governance structure, lack of technical expertise, and lack of funds for capital injection from the lead investor, led to the near collapse of the concession. Under the Concession Agreements, the concessionaire was required to (i) meet specified freight volume targets; (ii) meet the stipulated minimum investment in infrastructure and equipment; (iii) provide passenger services at specified frequencies and level of quality (for Kenya only); (iv) maintain the infrastructure and equipment to certain specified standards; (v) conform to the given minimum safety standards; and (vi) pay promptly the agreed concession fees. However, by 2010, the performance of RVR was well below specified targets, such that:

1. Freight volumes had not increased and remained below the concession baseline with a 7 percent shortfall in Kenya and a 10 percent shortfall in Uganda.
2. Investments in infrastructure in Kenya had been only approximately US$0.85 million against a minimum target of US$5 million, whereas in Uganda, it was about US$0.3 million against a minimum target of US$2 million.
3. In the case of passenger services in Kenya, the concessionaire had provided only 68 percent of the target.
4. Infrastructure and equipment had not been maintained as per the required standards, and as a result, had continued to deteriorate.
5. Safety standards had not been complied with in general.
6. Concession fees had not been paid in either country since January 2008. In Uganda, the amount due was approximately US$1 million; in Kenya, US$5 million.

As a result of nonperformance, the concessionaire was issued a termination notice. At the expiry of the notice, IFC and KfW, the main lenders, were signaled in January 2009 to begin the first 90 days of the cure period, as per the terms of the lenders' agreement.

Restructuring of the Concession

After a protracted period of negotiations and discussion of alternative ways to restructure the concession and bring in fresh investors, the Concession Agreements, including the Interface Agreement, were amended to allow new investors to buy shares in the new concession holding company. Citadel Group from the Arab Republic of Egypt, through its subsidiary Ambiance Ventures Ltd, bought out Sheltham and other shareholders except Transcentury, and with the help of IFC, agreement among all parties was reached on a new structure and financing plan.

The new structure involved creation of a new holding company—Kenya Uganda Railway Holdings (KURH). By June 2010, the shareholding of RVR group changed as follows: 51 percent by the Ambience Ventures (subsidiary of Citadel Group), 34 percent by Safari Rail (a subsidiary of Transcentury), and 15 percent by Ugandan investor Bomi Holdings Ltd. A share swap was made effective in October 2010, and the RVR shareholders swapped their shares for shares in KURH, the new lead investor.

Building Integrated Markets within the East African Community
http://dx.doi.org/10.1596/978-1-4648-0227-0

Current Operational Status

With the new shareholders and restructuring of the concession and a more detailed analysis of the condition of the track and the rolling stock, the project investment costs and the financing plan were revised. The required investment cost was estimated at US$311.0 million as opposed to the original estimate of US$111.0 million (table C.3).

Citadel Group, the majority shareholder, was able to pay off all the debt owed to the two governments and furthermore attracted renewed interest from other lenders to advance credit facilities up to US$164 million, including AfDB (US$40 million), Equity Bank (US$20 million), Netherlands Development Finance Company (FMO)/BIO (US$30 million), and IFC Debt Pool (US$20 million). This was in addition to the restructuring of the earlier balance of funding from IFC (US$22 million) and KfW (US$32 million). A technical management agreement was signed with América Latina Logística (ALL), a Brazilian logistics company, to provide technical advice and skilled manpower to operate the railway as needed (see box C.1). The new management team is in place and the debt funds from IFC, African Development Bank (AfDB), and KfW have started to flow (US$49.1 million in December 2011) after compliance with the conditions precedent, including completion of all environmental and social studies.

The IDA PRGs have been agreed and were soon to become effective at the time when this report was prepared. Retrenchment of excess staff has been completed and resettlement of project-affected persons is ongoing with World Bank assistance. A revised business plan is under implementation with ALL (Brazil) providing technical assistance, including staff, operational know-how, performance monitoring, training, planning and programming of infrastructure, and rolling stock rehabilitation. About 70 kilometers of track and drainage structures are under rehabilitation, and the rolling stock is being overhauled while new stock is on order. The lenders have appointed their "Engineer," who has already visited the site and begun supervision of works. While traffic volumes are yet to

Table C.3 Revised Project Cost and Financing Plan

Project cost	Amount ($m)	Project financing	Amount ($m)
Track	65.0	Equity	85.0
Locomotives	91.0	Debt	164.0
Wagons	89.0	Internal Cash Flow	62.0
Other (workshops, equipment, and so on)	16.0		
Total capital expenditures	261.0		
Other uses	50.0		
Total investment	**311.0**	**Total financing**	**311.0**

Source: World Bank.

Box C.1 The América Latina Logistica (ALL) Company and Its Role

América Latina Logística (ALL) is a Brazilian logistics company, focused on railway line logistics in Brazil. The largest company in Latin America in this sector, the company provides also transportation services such as logistics, intermodal transport, port operations, movement and storage of merchandise, administration of storage facilities, and general storage. It is also involved in leasing railroad equipment to third parties, and offers road transport services in Brazil through América Latina Logística Intermodal S.A.

The company was founded as Ferrovia Sul Atlântico in 1997 and is headquartered in Curitiba, Paraná state. Pursuant to a privatization process, it began operating lines in Paraná, Santa Catarina, and Rio Grande do Sul. It began operations in São Paulo state in 1998, and later (2001) acquired Delara Ltda, a Brazilian logistics company also operating in Argentina, Chile, and Uruguay. Operations were extended to Mato Grosso and Mato Grosso do Sul through acquisition in 2006.

The company assumed its current name after acquisition of its Argentine railway interests in 1999. There it partners with Railroad Development Corporation and the Argentine government in the operation of two freight services.

Under a Management and Technical support agreement entered into with the RVR Group of Companies, ALL is expected to offer RVR technical support for the next five years, supporting RVR in the management of the railway concessions in Kenya and Uganda. ALL is also required to assist in recruiting personnel and experts required to run the railway operations (financial managers, mechanics, track specialists, planning and control specialists, and human resource specialists). The staff to be provided by ALL are subject to approval by RVR and would be engaged by RVR as employees of the company reporting within the organizational structure.

ALL has a team based in Brazil to give support to the teams in Kenya. It will execute specific projects (consultancy projects/turnaround projects) that will be agreed with RVR and will train the local staff. Some of the key turnaround projects that will be implemented by ALL are as follows:

- Develop a balanced scorecard system; key performance indicators; cost control program; a diesel reduction program; and establishment and implementation of an operational and commercial performance monitoring routine and culture to achieve improved performance.
- Assist RVR to establish, prepare, and implement a plan for rehabilitation of infrastructure that reviews the condition of RVR's permanent infrastructure and prioritizes the rehabilitation works needed.
- Assist RVR to establish, prepare, and implement a plan for rehabilitation of RVR's rolling stock including wagons and locomotives.
- Assist RVR to identify and install new management structures and procedures to improve train planning/scheduling and control including, but not limited to, its train planning model; OCC routine and circulation; and train crew planning process and system.

box continues next page

Building Integrated Markets within the East African Community
http://dx.doi.org/10.1596/978-1-4648-0227-0

Box C.1 The América Latina Logística (ALL) Company and Its Role *(continued)*

- Assist RVR to establish and implement best practices in procurement including creation of synergies with ALL procurement procedures and, where possible, use of ALL's developed suppliers so as to benefit from economies of scale.
- Assist RVR to develop and implement a performance-oriented organizational culture and establish a training plan aimed at stimulating RVR staff to generate new ideas and solutions using tools of analysis and a strong statistical background to define, measure, analyze, implement, and control any particular situation.

pick up; the railway is carrying less than 5 percent of the total freight handled at the Mombasa port annually, this share is expected to increase to about 20 percent as the track is rehabilitated and the new rolling stack becomes operational.

Key Constraints and Challenges

The Kenya-Uganda Railway concession was the first of its kind in East Africa. It was initiated by Kenya and Uganda separately to privatize railway operations in their respective countries and the decision to privatize jointly as one concession was made midway when the two transaction advisers were almost ready to invite separate bids. Hence, the thinking that went into preparing the project as a regional project to be awarded to one concessionaire was rather limited. As a result, the exercise faced a number of constraints and challenges during preparation as well during implementation. Some of these constraints and challenges may be summarized as follows:

- There was no interlocutor at the regional level to coordinate and provide guidance to the preparation team. An ad hoc steering committee comprising representatives of the KRC and the URC; Ministers and Permanent Secretaries of the respective transport ministries; the privatization commissions of the two countries; the Ministries of Finance; representatives of the Attorney Generals; and other government officials and stakeholders had to be constituted to provide the platform for discussing issues and resolving differences. As a result, decisions took long to be made and there was not always consensus among different parties.
- The absence of a common regional legal and regulatory framework made it necessary to rely on an Interface Agreement to address cross-border issues and a temporary Joint Railway Commission that did not necessarily foresee or address problems that arose later during the implementation phase; nor did the Joint Commission have any legal powers to make its decisions binding since it was only an advisory body.
- The actual investment requirements (US$311 million), which turned out to be far greater than originally estimated (US$111 million), had serious implications on the required financial and managerial capability of the selected

concessionaire. The original concessionaire was unable to inject the necessary capital into the project or to meet the performance standards agreed in the concession.

- The original concession structure provided for a lead investor who would own 35 percent of the concession which could not be diluted until various conditions under the concession agreement were met. These conditions were stringent, unlikely to be met in the current framework to allow the speedy injection of additional equity.
- Assembling a large group of lenders and making amendments to concession agreements to satisfy various stakeholders (including two independent governments) without having a single authority to intervene when circumstances changed proved to be difficult and time consuming.
- The urge for expediency to reach financial close constrained due diligence on the condition of the track and rolling stock and the financial and managerial strength of the concessionaire; hence, there was an underestimation of the required investment and an overestimation of capability of the selected concessionaire. Standardization of concession agreements with respect to requiring clear specification of organizational structure for operating and managing the assets; a time-bound obligatory investment plan; and clearly measurable and relevant performance indicators would have reduced the risk of early failure of the concession.

Conclusions and Lessons Learned

The following conclusions and lessons can be drawn from the experience of the Kenya-Uganda railway concession, with special implications for the important role that the EAC can play to promote successful cross-border PPPs:

- Structuring future regional PPPs calls for much more extensive due diligence on the scope of work, investment estimates, required technical and management skills, and alternatives for overall organizational framework for management of concessions.
- To achieve successful PPPs at the regional level, EAC Partner States must have well-coordinated, harmonized, and complementary PPP policies.
- Common guidelines for the regional infrastructure subsectors should be adopted to cover: safety, financing, environmental management, local community participation, certification of sector personnel, operating licenses, consumer rights, remedies against noncompliance with contractual provisions, provision for key data collection and dissemination, and structuring of regional PPPs.
- Mechanisms at the EAC level should be developed for effective monitoring and evaluation of regional PPPs.
- The EAC can add value to regional PPPs by providing a platform for the development of greater standardization, including model concession agreements for regional projects and for improved mechanisms of dispute resolution.

- For a very large PPP project involving two or more countries, the EAC should consider setting up a special purpose regional entity (with appropriate shareholding by member states) to which would be assigned the assets to be concessioned, such that there is a single owner and a single concessionaire at the regional level, avoiding the need to develop several concession agreements.

Notes

1. The opening of the Mombasa-Nairobi refined products pipeline in the late 1970s took away a segment of the market, but KRC failed to utilize the released capacity to dominate the heavy oils market in the 1980s and 1990s.

2. Source: Surface and Marine Transport Regulatory Authority.

3. Esther Koimet, Investment Secretary, Ministry of Finance, Kenya.

Johannesburg to Maputo
N4 Toll Road Case

Introduction

In 2012, the N4 Toll Roll celebrated 15 years of what the participating governments view as highly successful implementation. The project was structured as a 30-year concession awarded in 1997 to the Trans Africa Concessions consortium (TRAC). The contract required the concessionaire to design, upgrade, construct, operate, and maintain the toll road before turning it back to the governments for operation after the 30-year term. The contract was estimated to be worth South African Rand 3 billion at the time the contract was signed (in excess of US$650 million in 1997 values). Half of that amount was required to be secured at the time of financial close to cover the costs of a three-year initial construction period.

When the project reached closure, it was recognized as a pioneering accomplishment—it was the first toll road concession signed in Sub-Saharan Africa. It was the first cross-border transport Public-Private Partnership (PPP), and only the second regional PPP in any sector.[1] It also became the first of several major PPP projects planned for the Maputo Development Corridor, which links South Africa's most industrialized, but effectively landlocked, northern and eastern regions (Gauteng and Mpumalanga provinces) to the Mozambican port of Maputo. In addition to the toll road, other PPPs of various kinds were expected to generate investment in rail lines, a border post, and seaport facilities. The infrastructure PPPs in turn were expected to make possible a host of industrial and commercial opportunities along the 590 kilometers route from Johannesburg to Maputo.

The toll road and the wider corridor initiative of which it was a key part were expected to become models for similar developments across the continent. But 15 years later, no new cross-border toll road concessions have been signed, only two national toll road concessions have reached closure outside of South Africa, and none of the dozen or so potential transport/trade corridors identified across the continent have come close to the sort of development achieved by the

Maputo Development Corridor (MDC). Finally, of the other PPPs planned for the MDC, only the port concession can be considered to have been a successful PPP project, but with some important qualifications.

The purpose of this case study is to explain how the N4 PPP project was developed and implemented, how successful it was, and why it seems to have been a unique project, extremely difficult to replicate. The N4 toll road is a successful, cross-border PPP. But in many respects it was not developed in ways that were particularly regional or cross-border in nature. Some of the questions that this project poses for Regional Economic Communities (RECs) are: (i) would this project have been more successful if it had been done with stronger regional participation; (ii) if this project were being developed today, could an REC add value to its development; and (iii) what kinds of resources (funding, skills, and so on) would be needed for an REC to play such a constructive role?

Context: The Maputo Corridor

The MDC

One of the first and biggest advantages the toll road had in terms of demonstrating bankability to potential private partners was the fact that it was a core element of a much bigger economic development effort, involving strong government support for hundreds of projects that would ensure steady increases in traffic levels along the road for many years to come. After the end of apartheid in 1994, South Africa and Mozambique began a process of rebuilding their relationship as southern Africa neighbors, and in 1995 began to formally discuss a strategy for revitalizing the Maputo Corridor, which had been an active trade and transport corridor between the two countries since the 1800s. The process was seen to involve several objectives that were quickly agreed to in the ongoing discussions between the two governments: (i) the rehabilitation of primary infrastructure along the corridor using private sector involvement; (ii) commercial investment in the various potential projects made possible by a rebuilt corridor; (iii) the generation of jobs and economic growth; and (iv) the development of policies and frameworks to facilitate holistic and participatory approaches to environmental management (Interim Co-ordinating Committee 1996). These objectives reflected what the two governments saw as a variety of different kinds of specific investment projects needed to reestablish the links between the two countries:

Private Sector Participation in the Rehabilitation of Primary Infrastructure

N4 toll road (Witbank to Maputo): The governments originally estimated that US$100 million in private investment was needed to rehabilitate 380 kilometers of existing road on the South African side of the border and the construction of 50 kilometers of new road in Mozambique. Another US$100 million would be needed to maintain the road over the 30-year lifespan of a contemplated toll road concession contract, so that at the end of the concession the governments would be handed back the road in good condition. This would be the first toll

Figure D.1 The N4 Route

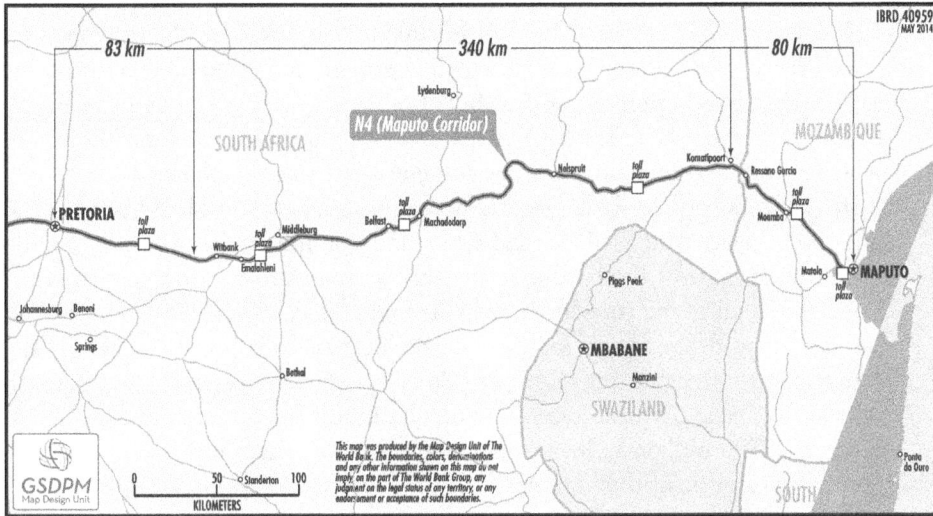

Source: TRAC.

concession ever attempted in Sub-Saharan Africa. In addition to being a core element of what was expected to be a revitalized transport and trade corridor, a second major advantage of the toll in terms of demonstrating bankability was that most of it was located in South Africa (figure D.1); most of it was already functioning and therefore would generate toll revenues relatively quickly.

Maputo port: A well-functioning port in Maputo was essential to anchor the eastern end of the corridor, to generate traffic for the road and railway, and to open access to the international economy. The government had already concessioned individual port facilities for containers and specific commodities, but improvements in overall port management and investments were desperately needed. The government assumed that US$170 million in new investment could be attracted via the kind of rehabilitate-operate-transfer (ROT) project it was contemplating for the rail line.

Railway links to Maputo: One of the keys to the redevelopment of the port was rehabilitation of the three railways that accessed it. All of these railways needed extensive rehabilitation of lines, signal equipment, and rolling stock after two decades of neglect and sabotage by the apartheid government in South Africa. The total cost of upgrading the 90 kilometers Mozambican segment of the Ressano Garcia line leading into Gauteng was estimated in the mid-1990s at US$100 million in line rehabilitation and new rolling stock. It was assumed that some measure of private investment for the railway could be attracted via a ROT project, possibly structured as a joint venture with the Mozambican government.

One-stop border post: To facilitate freight and passenger flows between the two countries, the two governments realized that a one-stop border control procedure was needed. In the mid-1990s, long processing delays at the border meant that even if the road and railway were rehabilitated, the route from Pretoria to

Maputo would not be competitive with routes from Pretoria to the South African ports of Durban and Richards Bay to the south. The design of such a facility was quickly prepared. It was estimated to cost US$30 million to construct over a three-year period. Private sector investment and operation was contemplated, via a build-operate-transfer (BOT) project.

Energy transmission: The one major infrastructure rehabilitation project in which private participation was not contemplated was the construction of two high-voltage electricity lines from Duvha (near Johannesburg) to Maputo. The lines were needed to facilitate industrial and commercial investments on the Mozambique side of the border. Again, this was part of the effort to strengthen the eastern end of the corridor, to help facilitate the east-west flow of goods and services along the road and railway. The project was to be implemented by the Mozambique Transmission Company, a joint venture partnership of South African, Swazi, and Mozambican electricity utilities. The project was expected to involve US$90 million in investment, about half of which was targeted for the South African side of the border.

Commercial Investments in the Corridor

On May 6, 1996, the presidents of the two countries, Nelson Mandela and Joaquim Chissano, jointly launched the MDC at an "investors' conference" in Maputo. Over 180 mostly commercial projects, purportedly worth over US$7 billion, were identified for private investment. Most of the projects on the list were not prepared or packaged to any significant degree, but the list did include some large projects already planned or under construction:

- The Mozal project, a US$1.4 billion aluminum smelter near Maputo, was already in development when the toll road bidding process began. BHP Billiton in a joint venture with the South African development bank, the Industrial Development Corporation (IDC), was planning to invest US$1.3 billion in a first phase of the project, which also had strong support from Eskom, the South African power utility. Its chances of success were already apparent—Mozal was similar to the Hillside smelter, completed in Richard Bay in 1996 by the same developers using the same technology. Hillside, completed four months early and 21 percent under budget, had already become the world's largest greenfield aluminum smelter. Mozal has gone on to be a hugely successful investment project. It has gone through several phases of investment and expansion to become anchor of the Maputo Development Corridor and a principal reason for the ongoing viability of the toll road;
- The Belulane Industrial Park, a 600 hectare industrial free zone, was being planned in an area adjacent to the Mozal plant—the zone was expected to attract a mix of foreign, regional, and local investors into heavy industry, manufacturing, and hi-tech businesses.
- A US$2 billion iron and steel complex in Matola (adjacent to the Maputo port), based on South African ore and Mozambican gas, was also being assessed at this time.

- The development of the Pande/Temane gas field in Mozambique and the construction of a pipeline to South Africa (US$1.4 billion) were being prepared by South Africa's parastatal gas utility, SASOL, and Mozambique's ENH.
- Many other smaller projects were identified in agriculture, mining, tourism, and manufacturing. A relatively small number of social infrastructure projects were also identified, most notably the water and sanitation scheme in the South African town of Nelspruit (in eastern Mpumalanga), which became a groundbreaking 30-year water concession, signed in 1999.

Political Economy: Accepting a Role for the Private Sector

With the election victory in 1994, the African National Congress (ANC) made a very clear, outspoken effort to portray South Africa as an attractive location for private sector investment, which was quickly formalized in government policy. At the 1996 investors' conference launching the corridor initiative, Nelson Mandela spoke of the need to "...maximize private sector participation, essential to the success of the project" (Mandela 1996).

One of the legacies faced by the ANC government was the profoundly unequal pattern of spatial development in South Africa. This pattern resulted in part from the fact that certain areas of the country had been disadvantaged by the import substitution industrial policy of the previous government, concentrating investments in areas based on their ability to service domestic requirements rather than in areas—like eastern Mpumalanga—more suited to export-oriented production. Exacerbating this spatial inequity was a huge backlog of infrastructure investment left for the ANC-led government to deal with after taking power. By 1997, there was an accumulated backlog for road infrastructure of R 37 billion, and in 1997 alone, the shortfall for road spending was R 4.7 billion (*Mail and Guardian* 2000). At the same time, the apartheid regime virtually exhausted the government resources needed to deal with such problems. The apartheid government increased the country's budget deficit from 0.9 percent of GDP in 1989/90 to 10.8 percent of gross domestic product (GDP) in 1993/94. In its last year of power, the government increased the national debt by 32 percent (R 60 million) (Taylor 2000).

So partnership with the private sector became an essential aspect of South African Spatial Development Initiative (SDI) policy, endorsed by the Cabinet in 1995. The promotion of SDIs was an expression of a kind of government-driven industrial policy, but the government was to have a limited role in implementing it. SDIs were conceived as private sector-driven initiatives, because due to fiscal constraints, "government's financial investment in an initiative is limited to less than 10 percent of the total amount" (Jourdan 1998). Government's responsibility was to point the private sector in the right direction and facilitate project preparation, but not to take on the full burden of project development.

The need to rely on the private sector for 90 percent of required investment was taken up with urgency by certain sectoral ministries. The South African Department of Transport (DOT) was the first sectoral ministry to formalize and prioritize the use of PPPs. DOT published a white paper in 1996 that strongly endorsed the use of PPPs like BOT toll road projects as mechanisms for addressing "fiscal constraints" (DOT 1996). By 1997, the South African Roads Board had prepared an aggressive policy for encouraging unsolicited bids from private companies as a way to increase the use of tolling to pay for the rehabilitation of regional roads.

In 1994, Frente de Libertação de Moçambique (Mozambique Liberation Front; FRELIMO) won the first elections and accelerated the transition to a market-based economy by driving an aggressive program of economic reforms, including the privatization of 900 state-owned enterprises and the removal of price controls on goods and services. The Mozambican president who drove the economic reforms, Joaquim Chissano, appeared with Nelson Mandela at the Maputo Corridor investors' conference in 1996 to invite private capital into the corridor.

Project Preparation

Several key characteristics distinguish the process of preparing the toll road concession and help account for its success.

High-Level Political Support

One of these characteristics was the degree of high-level political support for the MDC in general and the toll road in particular. In retrospect, it is hard to imagine how political support for the project could have been much stronger. And the support is understandable for several reasons:

- The newly elected ANC-led government was eager to demonstrate developmental successes, especially via high-profile investment projects that included job creation and social development.
- In addition to being Mozambique's ally in the liberation struggle, South Africa had strong economic interests in seeing its neighbor develop quickly—in 1997, the GDP in Mozambique was US$2 billion, compared to US$130 billion in South Africa (Driver and de Barros 2000). South Africa's own economic development would be hampered by having such a poor neighbor at its doorstep. And South African commercial interests saw many profitable opportunities in Mozambique—Eskom was particularly interested in helping to develop the country's vast hydropower potential.

President Nelson Mandela had long considered FRELIMO to be a strong ally of the ANC-led resistance in South Africa. Nothing better demonstrates Mandela's commitment to the corridor and the toll road than his personal appeal to private sector investors at the MDC launch in Maputo in 1996.

Thabo Mbeki was the executive face of government in South Africa from 1994–98 as vice president, then through two terms as president. He was also a key architect of a South African economic policy that was fiscally conservative, but pragmatic, focusing on controlling inflation, liberalizing trade, and facilitating Private Sector Development, all as a way of increasing job growth and household income. The MDC embodied many aspects of his approach to socioeconomic development, and Mbeki was a key factor in getting the various South African departments and parastatals to fall in line with the corridor idea.

Mathews Phosa was the first ANC premier of Mpumalanga province. He was one of the first four members of the ANC to return from exile in 1990 to begin negotiations with the apartheid government. Born in Nelspruit, a key promise of his campaign for office in 1994 was rehabilitation of the road between the provincial capital Nelspruit and Maputo port. He drove the toll road development process at the provincial level until he became a member of the ANC's National Executive Committee in 1999.

Mac Maharaj was the ANC government's first minister of transport, serving from 1994 to 1999. Maharaj was perhaps the best-known political "public face" of the toll road, meeting repeatedly with his Mozambican ministerial counterpart, Paulo Muxanga, and signing the key MDC agreements on behalf of the South Africa government, including the initial agreement in 1995 and the MDC Framework Agreement in 1996 with an ancillary protocol governing toll road operations.

Institutional Arrangements

Another key characteristic of the toll road project development was the set of institutional arrangements put in place to manage the process. The project was developed within what now seems like a bewildering web of overlapping SDI policy and technical committees operating at the provincial, departmental, national, and binational levels. By 1995, an SDI Unit had been created at the Development Bank of South Africa (DBSA), led by officials from the Department of Trade and Industry (DTI). But the MDC and particularly the toll road were viewed at the time primarily as a transport initiative, largely because most of the key infrastructure components—the road, railway, port, and so on—already existed in some form. Therefore, the early development of the toll road as a PPP was led by the DOT. The in-house DOT capacity seems to have given the toll road PPP advantages that PPPs in other sectors never had.

In 1995, the DOT established a mostly in-house technical team that helped structure the toll road project. The department also had a number of experienced technical experts who had structured several government-operated toll roads in the country. In 1980, the South African Parliament first authorized the Minister of Transport to issue bonds to finance road infrastructure. By 1996, five government tolling projects were operational. Tolls were typically set too low for the projects to pay 100 percent of debt service on the bonds, but South Africans became familiar with tolling early on. And even though the total road length involved was small (380 kilometers), DOT engineers used the projects as opportunities to estimate things like the vehicle traffic, toll tariffs, and annual growth rates necessary to make long-term private toll roads bankable (Copley and Shaw 2007).

Building Integrated Markets within the East African Community
http://dx.doi.org/10.1596/978-1-4648-0227-0

DOT also had support from the DBSA, the IDC, and the Council for Scientific and Industrial Research (CSIR), and used all of this expertise to help provide technical support to an interdepartmental working committee at the national level. Mozambique developed a similar interdepartmental working committee, but without South Africa's in-house capacity they had to draw on consultants for the technical work and interaction with the South African experts.

In 1996, the South African DOT assisted in establishing a technical unit in Mpumalanga, providing funding for a technical support program at the provincial level. The purpose of this unit was to take over the actual day-to-day development of corridor projects once high-level policies and priorities had been agreed to by the two governments. But this "exit" by national-level South African officials never effectively took place because (i) the desire to speed the process along meant that national-level officials were uncomfortable relinquishing control to local officials; (ii) provincial officials lacked the skills and resources to take on these responsibilities; (iii) changes occurred in the nature of provincial political support for the corridor, with the assumption of office by politicians with different priorities from those of their predecessors who had championed the corridor; and (iv) with even less capacitated local officials, Mozambique did not establish a similar local unit and maintained a highly centralized approach to corridor activities, making it more difficult for South African local government officials to act effectively as counterparts.

Two new institutional mechanisms were established on July 26, 1996, to prepare and manage the toll road development process. In an effort to "speed up" the MDC process (which had been launched by the two presidents in Maputo two months earlier), the South African Transport Minister and the Mozambican Minister of the Department of Roads and Bridges (DNEP) signed a Framework Agreement for the establishment of the MDC, with several ancillary protocols. The first protocol stated a joint intention to establish a bi-national promotional entity, the Maputo Corridor Company (MCC), which would be a single entity consolidating and representing the corridor interests of the two countries, along with the private sector, and other key stakeholders. It was supposed to (i) provide strategic information on socioeconomic issues, planning, infrastructure, and financial matters; (ii) facilitate investment for trade, industry, and development within the corridor, and; (iii) identify constraints to the development of the corridor and lobby the relevant authorities to remedy those constraints (de Beer 2011).

A second protocol signed by the two ministers stated an agreement to create an Implementing Authority (IA) to prepare the toll road concession contract documentation and handle the tender process for selecting a private operator. The idea was to have one government counterpart for the private operator/sponsor, to simplify and streamline contract negotiations, construction oversight, and progress reporting.

Fast-track Implementation

A third characteristic of the project development process was made possible by the high-level political support and DOT's in-house capacity—fast-track, top-down implementation. This approach was adopted largely out of a desire to avoid the delays typical of normal public sector development planning and project preparation, and to save money by allocating more of the preparation work to the private sector. Reducing the costs of preparation for government was also important, because budgets were tight—lack of government resources was a principal reason for selecting a PPP approach in the first place.

The result was a highly centralized process characterized by a dominant role taken by national government officials, particularly those at South Africa's DOT as they developed the toll road project. Some notable results of this approach included the following:

- Toll road bids were called for before Mozambique had a legal framework allowing such projects.
- Bids were requested before the Implementing Authority was established.
- A publicly advertised request for expressions of interest was rejected in favor of a desktop exercise undertaken by DOT staff to prequalify five potential bidders who were then invited to submit initial bids.
- Local officials, much less local residents, were not consulted about many details of the project, including the toll tariff framework. Most South African and Mozambican local officials had not been involved in preparing the list of 180 projects offered to the private sector at the Maputo investors' conference in 1996, and reportedly were unhappy about being left out of the process (Mitchell 1998). Other local officials claimed that the national government had denied them access to the contract (Taylor 2000).

The process of moving from tender invitations to financial close was concluded between March 1996 and June 1998. This was unusually fast for a project of this size.

Project Structure

The main responsibilities for toll road development in a typical PPP include design, construction, maintenance, toll collection, arranging financing, and legal ownership. The build-operate-transfer (BOT) model is the most common approach used in assigning responsibilities for toll road projects and the N4 toll road is usually cited as an example of BOT. But the general term covers a number of subcategories including greenfield projects like build-own-operate-transfer (BOOT) and build-lease-transfer (BLT), as well as brownfield projects like rehabilitate-operate-transfer (ROT), lease-rehabilitate-operate (LRO), and build-rehabilitate-operate-transfer (BROT). The N4 is an example of this last subcategory, typically used to describe a project in which a private entity takes over the management of existing government-owned road assets and also assumes significant risk for investments needed to extend, complete, rehabilitate, and maintain the assets. The N4 was much more of a brownfield rehabilitation than a greenfield project. This helped account for strong private sector perceptions of bankability, because traffic flows could be estimated with some accuracy and risks associated with major construction had already been dealt with.

TRAC was created as a special-purpose entity by the French construction multinational Bouygues and South African construction companies Basil Read and Stocks & Stocks. By signing the N4 concession contract, TRAC agreed to finance, build, rehabilitate, maintain, and operate a facility for 30 years. After that period, the responsibility for the facility is to be transferred back to the governments. DBSA engineers explained the significance of the 30-year contract term by saying that over a 20-year period a road could function adequately with just routine maintenance. But 30 years would require significant rehabilitation over the last decade of that period, ensuring that the government received back a road in virtually new condition (Copley and Shaw 2007).

The two governments remain legal owners of the land on which the N4 was built. But TRAC owns the equipment used in constructing and maintaining the road for the life of the contract and is solely responsible for upgrading the road and maintaining it, and rebuilding sections of it, in return for revenue earned from tolls taken at five (eventually six) toll plazas along the road, which TRAC was also responsible for designing, locating, and constructing. After the concession period the road will be transferred back to the governments, who may decide to implement another concession agreement. In other words, TRAC has 30 years to recoup the cost of its investment and ongoing maintenance, plus make a commercial return, from revenue earned exclusively from tolls.

Contracting arrangements: Three contracts are central in a typical road concession. The concessionaire is hired pursuant to a concession contract, and then hires a construction company to act as the principal contractor in carrying out initial construction and rehabilitation of the facility assets pursuant to a construction contract. The concessionaire also normally engages an independent party (the operator) to operate and maintain the project on the terms and conditions specified in an operations and maintenance contract. Figure D.2 displays the overall structure of the N4 toll road BROT.

Construction companies often play leading roles in such consortia, and favor arrangements that maximize the contractor profits to be earned during the early stages of the concession. This was the case with the N4. The three original TRAC sponsors were construction companies whose main interest was the initial construction period. By the time the concession contract was signed, the three companies owned 40 percent of TRAC with nonsponsor investors contributing 6 percent of TRAC's equity (box D.1). TRAC hired Stocks and Stocks, Basil Read and Bouygues (SBB), a joint venture 100

Figure D.2 BROT Project Structure

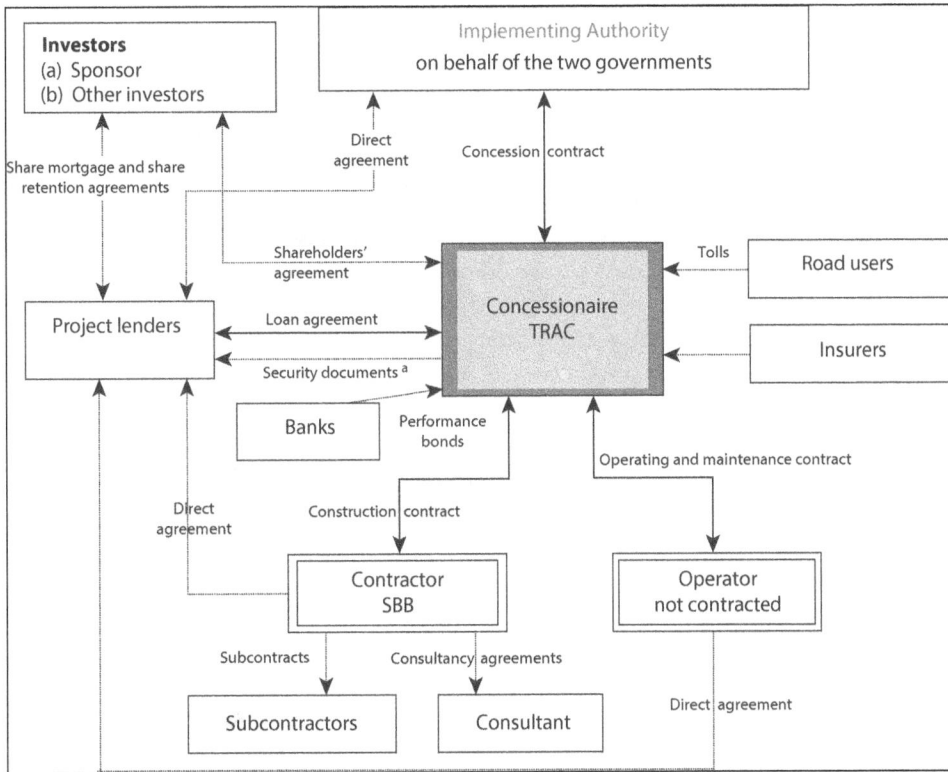

Source: Adapted from PADECO 1999.
a. Assignment of Concession Contract; Assignment of Construction Contract; Assignment of Operation &
Maintenance Contract; Charges over Bank Accounts; Liens & Pledges over Movable Property; Mortgages over
Land; Assignment of Insurances; Assignment of Performance Bonds.

percent owned by the three construction companies, to undertake the initial
construction work.

Rather than hire an independent company to act as operator, TRAC decided
to handle the operations and maintenance work itself, so it took on the responsibilities of the operator. The sponsoring construction companies had little interest
in staying with the project to do the operation and maintenance (O&M) work,
but the remaining owners of TRAC hired some of the contractor staff who had
been involved in the initial construction phase. Box D.2 details N4-related contracts and contractors.

Special contract requirements: The concession contract required that most of
the road undergo selective upgrading and rehabilitation, but TRAC also agreed
to build a new road to cover the last 50 kilometers from Moamba to Maputo,
cutting 20 kilometers off the route. The new construction and maintenance on
the 90 kilometers stretch of the road on the Mozambique side of the border

---

Box D.1 TRAC's Financiers

Equity (Sponsors/construction companies)
Bouygues (Fr)
Basil Read (SA)   **40% of TRAC (concessionaire)**
Stocks & Stocks (SA)   **100% of SBB (contractor)**

Equity (Non-sponsors)

20% of   South African Infrastructure Fund (SA)
total   Rand Merchant Bank Asset Management (SA)
                   Commonwealth Development Corporation (UK)
                   South African Mutual Life Assurance (SA)
                   Metropolitan Life Ltd (SA)
                   Sanlam Asset Management (SA)
                   SCDM (Moz)

Debt (excluding equity investors who also provided debt)
                   ABSA Corporate and Merchant Bank (SA)
80% of   Development Bank of Southern Africa (SA)
total   First National Bank (SA)
                   Mine Employees and Officials Pension funds (SA)
                   Nedcor Bank (SA)
                   Standard Corporate and Merchant Bank (SA)

Source: National Treasury 2001.

---

accounted for a third of the project's total costs, but only 7 percent of its revenues, suggesting that South African motorists were in effect cross-subsidizing their Mozambican counterparts (Taylor 2000).

A key aspect of TRAC's bid, which helped account for its success, was the inclusion in the project of a parallel 80 kilometers portion of road which could be developed to carry passenger vehicles around a constantly congested section of the N4 which could not be widened because it transversed a pass through the Mpumalanga escarpment on the western side of Nelspruit. This bypass was through an undulating geography that was unsuitable for trucks, so the traditional N4 route was to become the route of choice for heavy vehicles, and the more scenic bypass was favored by passenger vehicles.

An important part of the contract for the two governments was a requirement that TRAC generate socioeconomic project outcomes pursuant to a "social contract" with the Implementing Authority. These outcomes focused mainly on the empowerment and upliftment of communities in the immediate vicinity of the toll road through social and entrepreneurial development, job creation, job training, and skills transfer in a variety of fields, but especially in construction. These requirements were detailed in the contract and TRAC subsequently fulfilled most of its social contract obligations, but critics of the project have argued that

---

Box D.2   Selected TRAC Contracts and Contractors

Primary Contracts	Contracting Parties
1. Concession	Implementing Authority (IA) and TRAC
2. Construction	TRAC[a] and SBB[b]
3. Operations & maintenance	[TRAC retained this work]

Other contracts	Contracting Parties
4. Computerized tolling systems	TRAC and Tollink
5. Independent Engineer[c] (to administer primary contracts)	IA/TRAC and five consulting engineers (ASCH, Cotop-Eteng JV, Halcrow, Ninham Shand, Vela VKE)
6. Lenders Technical Advisor[d]	Lenders and Gibb Ltd/Gibb Africa JV
7. Civil engineering	SBB and civil engineering consultants JV (SNA, Bradford Conning, CPP, Bergman Ingerrop)

Notes:
a. TRAC was 40 percent owned by Stocks & Stocks, Bouygues, and Basil Read.
b. SBB was 100 percent owned by Stocks & Stocks, Bouygues, and Basil Read.
c. 40 percent of the IE costs were for TRAC's account.
d. 100 percent of the LTA costs were for TRAC's account.

Source: National Treasury 2001.

---

the concessionaire did the minimum necessary to meet these requirements and sustainable social change did not result.

Financing Arrangements

Financial structure: The concession was estimated to be worth approximately R 3 billion (about US$660 million in 1996). A total of R 1.5 billion was allocated for the initial three-year construction period and was required to be available at financial close. The second half was an estimate of the amount that would be needed later to pay for O&M over the lifetime of the concession. Much of this second half was expected to come from toll revenues. Financing for the project was split between 20 percent equity and 80 percent debt. Box D.3 indicates the financing structure of the initial financing allocation.

The three construction companies provided R 132 million of the equity (40 percent of the equity and 8 percent of total financing), and the remaining equity was contributed by the South African Infrastructure Fund, Rand Merchant Bank Asset Management, and five other investors. The debt component came from South Africa's four major banks and the DBSA. In 2005, the concessionaire successfully refinanced the project, substantially reducing the financial risk for the business, and enabling some expansion work to begin sooner than anticipated.

Box D.3 TRAC Financing Structure

			Millions of ZAR
Equity (20%):			
Sponsors	R	132	
Nonsponsors	R	199	
	R	331	

Debt (80%):			Term (years)	Grace on Principal (years)	Interest Rate
Rand term	R	469	15	4	2.125% over SA bank discount rate
CPI-linked	R	455	20	4	6% coupon subject to CPI indexation
DBSA	R	200	20	10	2.125% over SA bank discount rate
Subordinated	R	200	15	5	3% over SA bank discount rate
	R	1 324			

Total financing: R 1 655 (additional R 175 in standby debt available, conditional on additional equity)

Source: National Treasury 2001.

A major issue in the contract negotiations was the preferred bidder's insistence that the government provide revenue guarantees for the toll road, already a common feature of many toll roads in developing countries at this time (Fisher and Babbar 1996). The governments had already made much of public promises to pass on all financing risks to the concessionaire, so this issue was not quickly decided. But to avoid a collapse of negotiations with TRAC,[2] the governments compromised in the end. Government spokesmen were quick to point out that they had provided no government subsidies for the project. But both governments did eventually agree to provide joint and severable guarantees of the project debt and, under certain conditions, the equity as well.[3]

Expected rates of return: South African officials derived standard rates of return required for different kinds of private and Development Finance Institution (DFI) investments. These estimates were used in anticipating financing structures on two subsequent successful (national) private toll roads in South Africa, the N3 Toll Road (R 2.2 billion) and the Platinum Toll Road (R 3.3 billion). In general, it was concluded that on the N4, equity investors had sought a rate of return commensurate with perceived country risk. In South Africa in the mid-1990s, this was about 20 percent per year over a five-year time horizon. Commercial lenders looked for about 75 percent of that return, namely 15 percent over an eight-year horizon, with merchant banks targeting 60 percent of the equity return over 12 years (12 percent). The pensions funds sought 50 percent of the equity return over a 15-year horizon (10 percent), and DFI's linked their lending to floating rates, or to the cost of capital plus a margin, over 20-year horizons (Copley and Shaw 2007).

To ensure these targeted rates of return, the availability of cash for expansion works was subordinated to a minimum dividend paid to investors. This provided comfort for the lenders and investors on what was the first contract of its kind in Sub-Saharan Africa. But such an arrangement made it important to ensure that the work carried out in the initial construction period was of a quality to ensure that no unexpected remedial interventions would be required early in the concession period. This became an issue of concern on the N4, because the contractor was committed only for a 12-month defects liability period. As explained in more detail below, the governments' willingness to allow a fast-track approach to construction, plus the dominance of construction companies in the concession structure, led to a considerable number of construction defects in the initial construction period. Correction of these latent defects without diminishing the funding available for expansion of works meant that the contractor had to be willing to extend its latent defects cure period. Negotiating this was difficult because the contractors played a dominant role in the concessionaire. But eventually the contractors did work well beyond the latent defects period to fix problems.

Legal and Regulatory Issues

As noted above, South Africa first passed legislation allowing road tolling in 1980, on the basis of which five government-operated toll roads were implemented prior to the N4. Subsequent legislative changes allowed private companies to collect tolls and eliminated a requirement that motorists always have access to an alternative free road of a condition matching that of the toll road. In 1996, South Africa's DOT published its White Paper, which laid the policy groundwork for private toll road concessions.

At the time of the invitation for bids, there was no legislative framework for toll road concessions in Mozambique. The decision of the Mozambican government to pursue the toll road preceded the legal regime permitting the creation of toll roads and concessioning to private operators. But the government quickly took action to pass appropriate legislation just 10 days before the South African Transport Minister and his Mozambican counterpart signed the Framework Agreement establishing the MDC, with an ancillary protocol for operating the toll road (SADC Banking Association 2003).[4]

The setting of toll tariffs is the key area of ongoing toll road regulatory activity by governments. In the case of the N4, tolling had become a considerable source of controversy even before the contract was signed. The concession was initially based on toll tariffs set jointly by the National Roads Agency, TRAC, and TRAC's lenders and shareholders. The initial tariffs were R 0.20 per kilometers for light vehicles and R 0.50 per kilometers for heavy vehicles, and the contract stipulated that tariffs could only increase with the consumer price index (CPI). These rates were not usually high for South Africa, but commuters and other local users complained that they were suddenly being required to pay for trips to nearby schools and jobs. Users on the Mozambican side of the border were considerably poorer than those on the South African side and tended to be much less able to pay. Protests led to a decision by the concessionaire to establish a discount system that sharply reduced tariffs for some local users on both sides of the border.

The lack of basic public safety on the road was also an issue unforeseen at the time of contract signing. Criminal activity, including carjacking, rose substantially on the N4 beginning in the mid-1990s, and ordinary police resources were inadequate to deal with the problem. The concessionaire finally agreed to pay for special services, including 24-hour motorist assistance patrols, and special police patrols, as well as police vehicles for use on such patrols, to deal with safety issues on the road and justify the toll tariffs to local users.

Finally, both the government and the concessionaire failed to identify the unusual thinness of the road paving as a potential long-term problem for the concession (Alexander et al. 2004). In addition, neither the governments nor the concession agreement specified regulations for truck loading. It quickly became apparent to TRAC that overloaded trucks were damaging the roadway as soon as sections could be rehabilitated. To deal with this problem, the concessionaire began working with both governments to establish axle load control measures. The project, which became operational in 2002 and cost TRAC R 120 million, consisted of a set of six traffic control centers, equipped with measurement equipment to weigh axle loads. These were complemented by mobile units that could be dispatched to predetermined lay-by areas where they could identify overloaded trucks. The concessionaire reported that from 2001 to 2004, overloaded trucks as a share of all trucks dropped from 23 percent to 9 percent (UNDP 2008).

Safeguard Issues

One of the four overall objectives of the MDC involved safeguard issues: "To ensure sustainability by developing policies, strategies and frameworks that ensure a holistic, participatory and environmentally sustainable approach to development" (Interim Co-Coordinating Committee 1996). But the fast-track, top-down approach used in development of the toll road project undercut the willingness and ability of project proponents to meet this objective. The project was not developed along what now would be considered conventional steps, involving a series of activities undertaken and assessed before a decision could be made about whether or not to proceed with implementation. Normally these steps would include an appraisal of likely environmental, economic, technical and social impacts, plus consultation with communities and other stakeholders likely to be affected by the project.

The SDI approach used by the South African government severely shortened the time available for assessing environmental impacts in order to meet implementation milestones. The DOT set extremely tight deadlines for the production by TRAC of an environmental impact assessment (EIA) of the toll road, and the Mpumalanga provincial government had little time to evaluate it. By mid-1998, as construction got under way, TRAC and the environmental regulator found themselves in a position of having to work with local communities already hostile to aspects of the toll road.

When the corridor project was launched in 1996, there was a limited statutory basis for the government to require EIAs from developers proposing development schemes. While one of the stated goals of the corridor was to develop an environmentally sustainable framework for development, it was not until September 1997 that the provincial government could require EIAs for major projects such as roads, railway lines, and power infrastructure. (Of course by this time, TRAC and the Implementing Authority had already signed the concession agreement.) It was April 1998 before EIAs were required for smaller developments such as hotel and industrial projects. By mid-1998, the provincial government had initiated a series of environmental and sector-planning studies to assess the likely impacts of the corridor and some of its projects already under way, and to begin the process of developing the sustainable framework for future development. But the toll road construction was well under way before the provincial regulator had the ability to ensure socially and environmentally sustainable outcomes.

Shortcomings of Project Preparation

The fast-track, top-down project implementation strategy, driven mostly by the South African government, created problems as well as benefits for the toll road project. The process was meant to save time and avoid delays. It was also meant to cut government costs by allocating to the private sector some of the preparation activities that presumably they could perform better, faster, and cheaper than government. But the process resulted to a significant extent in a false economy in terms of fast-tracking development because it led to a variety of problems later during implementation.

Tendering problems: One problem with this approach was that government officials thought they could use the bidding process to force the prospective private partners to do most of the project preparation work involving feasibility assessments and detailed project design. But this turned out to be a highly unrealistic expectation. South Africa's DOT team understood much about the engineering side of toll roads, but relatively little about PPPs. They knew that one of the keys to bidding out PPPs of this nature was to maximize private sector innovation by specifying project outputs in the bid documents and letting bidders propose project inputs. But they misunderstood how far this concept could be taken. It is now widely acknowledged that to avoid radically different proposals that are difficult to compare, in practice project design is a shared responsibility, with the public sector taking the lead in the preliminary design (for a road this would include route alignment, number of lanes, interchanges, and other high-level design specifications). The private sector would then complete the design, subject to government approval.

DOT officials later admitted that because of self-imposed time constraints and a desire to shift work to the bidders, the N4 tender documentation did not define the project in adequate detail and required bidders to do too much of the detailed design. This made the tendering process particularly difficult for bidders, since each had to assess exactly what it would offer to construct to meet relatively vague government requirements, and to price these works and provide the necessary project finance. As with similar PPPs developed in the mid-1990s, the DOT team thought they were ensuring that bidders would do most of the critical feasibility assessments and design work by warning that changes in the contract would not be allowed later because of design amendments or mistakes in preparation. The N4 bidders were told that errors in assumptions could not be offset by tariff increases during implementation—once set at contract signing, tariffs would only be increased in line with CPI. This made the N4 project particularly risky for bidders as construction price increases can differ substantially from changes in the CPI.[5]

So while bidders did not want to pay for full design work for tender submissions, they could not afford to take too many chances with their proposals. Most of them hired consulting engineers to do a substantial amount of preliminary design and technical work. In addition, financial, legal, and commercial work was done by other experts hired by the bidding consortia. By the time the final bids were submitted, the lump sum fixed prices offered for the initial construction work were in most cases based on a substantial amount of preliminary design work by experts who had been hired for bid preparation, but who had little or no expected involvement in an eventual concession contract (Alexander et al. 2004).

To the extent that bidders responded with detailed proposals, the government evaluation team had problems comparing and contrasting them because they were based on different design assumptions. The evaluators eventually prepared their own base case scenario against which to compare the different offerings and assess value for money. One of DBSA's senior engineers estimated that the governments had paid R 32 million to prepare what was in effect their own bid for the project (Copley and Shaw 2007).

But most of the bid designs were presented in outline form and lacked precise definitions of what the tenderers were actually offering. This led to more complications in tender evaluation and contract negotiation, as well as a significant number of disputes during actual construction. The experience ultimately generated some benefits for the governments. South African National Roads Agency Limited (SANRAL) modified its bidding procedures for subsequent toll roads, taking more time for preparation of preliminary designs and requiring bidders to specify in more detail exactly what they were offering to do in each year of the contract, in a matrix format, with each element priced separately (Alexander et al. 2004).

Construction problems: Another problem with the fast-track approach was that it assumed that the eventual N4 concessionaire would have a long-term interest in the viability of the project. But in the case of TRAC, the concession structure was dominated by the sponsoring construction companies, and these firms had interests and expectations that were somewhat different from what the governments had anticipated.

TRAC's nonsponsor investors recognized that the primary interest of the three sponsoring construction companies was in the profits they would make building and rehabilitating the road, and that they had no interest in future operations and maintenance. So to add some incentives for the contractors to consider the longer-term sustainability of their work, the other investors required that these sponsors maintain their equity position in TRAC for a minimum period of time. But the agreement locked in those firms for only four years—the three years of construction plus a one-year defects correction period. In fact, within six years after the signing, all of the construction companies had sold off their share holdings.

Given the fact that construction companies dominated the concession structure, the fast-track approach led to a series of construction problems, which SANRAL took steps to avoid on later toll roads projects. To save time in construction, for example, the N4 concession documentation allowed self-certification of construction quality by the contractor. In other words, the contractor could supervise its own work and make its own decisions regarding the acceptability of the completed work, with relatively little oversight required by anyone. Therefore, when disputes arose regarding the compliance with specifications, the disputes were generally resolved in a fashion that favored the contractor.

In addition, incentive bonus clauses for early completion of the works were included in the construction contract to allow the concessionaire to begin tolling as soon as possible. In a number of cases, this led to hasty construction and inadequate attention to quality. The contractor used a European approach to quality assurance, which minimized the number of quality supervisors on site. Neither the design engineer nor the independent supervising engineer (IE) (who reported jointly to the IA and concessionaire) had enough authority to adequately influence the standard of work on the project. Most of the South African construction personnel involved were used to having work approved by independent quality supervisors, rather than via self-certification. The result of applying all of this on the N4 projects was "poor quality work" in the view of SANRAL (Alexander et al. 2004).

Problems with longer-term project viability: Given a concession structure dominated by private companies having only a three- to five-year interest in a 30-year project, it can be a mistake to attempt to force them take on most of the responsibility for thorough feasibility assessments, detailed design work, or even defect-free construction that pays adequate attention to the long-term viability of the project. After 15 years, it is difficult to know exactly what other project problems can be attributed to the combination of fast-track approach and contractor-dominated concession, but all of the following were problems on the N4 project, and all of these could owe their existence to this combination:

- Overly optimistic traffic forecasts—of all the forecasts done by the government, lenders, and contractor, the latter were the most optimistic.
- Failure to anticipate resistance to tolls—the concessionaire claimed to have done some surveys, but obviously did not detect the kind of anger manifested once tolling began.

- Failure to anticipate road safety issues—the need to sponsor safety patrols and purchase police vehicles proved to be a significant longer-term expense for the concessionaire.
- Failure to recognize road thickness problems—this is a standard toll road feasibility issue that both the government and the concessionaire should have recognized early on.
- Failure to notice the lack of government regulations on truck loading—correcting this problem cost the concessionaire R 120 million.

This list is similar to the checklists of project "red flags" developed in the wake of the Asian crisis in other regions to identify projects that were highly susceptible to delays, protracted negotiations, renegotiations, and cancellations (Fitch Ratings 2009; Monsalve 2009;). The fact that none of these larger problems affected the N4 is testimony to the strength of its project success factors, discussed later.

Regional Aspects of the Project

Historically and geographically speaking, the N4 was a regional project, but in terms of management and governance, it was developed much more like a national project.

A Long History of Trade and Transport

The N4 may have been a groundbreaking "regional" project in the sense that it was the first road PPP project of any kind in Sub-Saharan Africa to involve more than one country. But the geographical trade/transport connection between the Port of Maputo and Gauteng, South Africa's industrial heartland, existed long before officials of the two government met in 1995 to talk about a development corridor. In other words, the corridor had long had an important regional dimension in the sense of linking the two countries with a trade and transport conduit. As the shortest route to an export harbor for South Africa's major industries, the link from Johannesburg to Maputo made geographic and economic sense, and by the 1970s, 40 percent of the exports from this region of South Africa went through Maputo. But traffic volumes collapsed and the infrastructure deteriorated beginning with Mozambique's independence in 1975 and the devastating civil war that followed, which reportedly claimed over 900,000 lives and US$15 billion in damages and lost production (Taylor 2000). Sanctions against the apartheid government in South Africa reduced trade flows to the Maputo port, but even those flows stopped when South Africa began efforts to sabotage Mozambican infrastructure assets as part of a program to destabilize what they considered to be a dangerous Marxist government on their border. After the end of apartheid, the two governments were eager to begin reestablishing the historical trade and travel links that had tied them together for 100 years, prior to the late 1970s.

Building Integrated Markets within the East African Community
http://dx.doi.org/10.1596/978-1-4648-0227-0

A Role for SADC?

Some commentators have argued that a third regional characteristic of the toll road helped account for its success: the fact that it was consistent with regional initiatives and priorities promoted by the Southern Africa Development Community (SADC) (UNDP 2008). SADC was founded in 1980 by nine southern African countries, including Mozambique. It began with four objectives: (i) to reduce the dependence of member states on the apartheid government in South Africa (not a SADC member until the end of apartheid in 1994); (ii) to implement programs and projects with regional impacts; (iii) to mobilize resources of members states to promote collective self-reliance; and (iv) to secure international understanding and support for the southern Africa region.

In 1996, SADC ratified two protocols intended to establish an environment for the development of regional trade and transport projects, which some have claimed helped with the N4 project. The Trade Protocol of 1996 called for the elimination of trade barriers among the member countries by 2005. The Protocol on Transport, Communications, and Meteorology encouraged private sector involvement, PPPs, and regional integration for a number of purposes:

- Revitalization of regional transport and trade links
- Rehabilitation and improvement of transport infrastructure
- Deregulation of ports, railways road agencies, and airlines/airports
- Harmonization of transport rules and trade regimes
- Facilitation of border controls through one-stop border posts and cross-border road transport agencies

Clearly the SDI program, driven mainly by the South African DOT, targeted objectives that were consistent with SADC's aim to facilitate regional economic cooperation. But the toll road, as well as the wider corridor development process, was implemented outside of the SADC framework on a narrowly bilateral basis that in effect excluded other regional SADC members. South Africa had already initiated something similar with the Lesotho Highlands Water Project, a bilateral water project designed to provide Lesotho with a source of income (and hydropower generation resources) in exchange for the provision of water to support mining and industrial activity in central Gauteng.

In general, South Africa seems to have deliberately kept the development of the toll road and the corridor on a bilateral basis, in order to maintain the fast track approach and avoid disputes around private investment projects. SADC officially endorsed the idea of PPPs but some of its members were still uncomfortable with such projects. Through the 1990s, aggressive South African businesses and parastatal enterprises attracted regional mistrust and caution. Much of this tension with SADC dissipated as the corridor work unfolded and the industrial projects took shape in Mozambique.

Regional Project Developed Largely by One Country

The toll road was indeed a bilateral, cross-border project, but much of the speed with which it reached successful financial closure is attributable to the fact that it was developed and managed in the style of a single, national project. The original concept of the toll road was to maintain a single cross-border facility as the administrator of the road. And the Implementing Authority was established to serve this purpose. But the process from the beginning was dominated by South African politicians, financiers, in-house technical expertise, and above all, DOT's fast-track, top-down approach to project development. Critics complained that stakeholders were not engaged in project planning, and many critics included the Mozambican government among those neglected stakeholders. But the reality of the toll road was that the South African stretch of the road was expected to generate 94 percent of the revenues, and allow almost immediate tolling because the South African stretch of road was already functioning (Copley and Shaw 2007).

The IA lasted two years, roughly until construction started. The governments quickly concluded that two separate authorities were needed because the countries used two different legal systems (Roman Dutch Law in South Africa and Portuguese Colonial Law in Mozambique), as well as different systems for taxation, currency management, and company reporting. In April 1998, South Africa created a state-owned company, the South African National Road Agency Ltd (SANRAL). A year later, the Mozambican government created a counterpart to SANRAL, known as Administracao Nacional de Estradas (ANE). Administration of the toll road on behalf of the two governments was transferred from the IA to the two new companies.

The Maputo Corridor Company (MCC), created in 1997 to consolidate and represent the interests of public and private corridor stakeholders, lasted a bit longer than the IA, but never really achieved any of its objectives. Designed to be a not-for-profit company with shareholding by the public and private sectors, the MCC began its operations with a deputy Chief Executive Officer (CEO) appointed by South Africa and a one-year budget provided by the South African DOT (Mozambique was supposed to appoint and pay for the CEO). But legal restrictions in Mozambique made the non-profit status of the MCC difficult to achieve and the private sector was not enthusiastic about sharing ownership with the governments. A decision was taken in mid-1998 to limit the MCC to a public sector initiative with separate project managers in Nelspruit and Maputo and separate budgets provided by the respective departments of transport. By 2000, the South African government was growing fatigued with the MCC's lack of accomplishment and in 2001 withdrew its support, transferring the balance of MCC funding to the Mpumalanga provincial government for corridor activities.

Current Operational Status

The Toll Road: Successful Against the Odds

In a construction period lasting 38 months, the initial rehabilitation of the existing road and the construction of the new road portion in Mozambique were completed, with five toll stations in operation. Almost all of the 37 sections of the route required some work. By March 2001, the link into the Port of Maputo had also been completed. In mid-2002, weighbridges were completed in South Africa, followed by weighbridges in Mozambique in 2004, to control truck loading and ensure appropriate revenue collection. In 2004, the project was extended to include the N4 road sections between Witbank and Pretoria, adding almost another 200 kilometers to the original 440 kilometers (but the original 30-year term of the contract was not changed).

The construction program was scheduled for 43 months, excluding a defects liability period. The contractor completed the work with five months to spare to earn early completion bonuses and allow tolling to begin early. But as noted above, the correction of latent defects delayed final completion by another 25 months.

SANRAL eventually concluded that construction quality control for most of the contract proved to be inadequate. But in terms of project outcomes, the toll road has been a success. Cross-border road freight grew from 29,000 tons in 1997 to an estimated 1.2 million tons in 2006, with about 65 percent of the flow consisting of goods moving from South Africa to Mozambique. By 2007, passenger transport between the two countries, mostly over the road, had increased by 80 percent since the lifting of visa requirements between the two countries in April 2005.

By 2007, TRAC employed over 400 full-time staff and supported over 60 local enterprises as subcontractors. The project's contribution to small business development already had been significant, with 702 contracts in construction with a value of US$38 million, 6,220 permanent, temporary, and casual jobs, and 20,260 people having received job training through various programs (de Beer 2011). Critics have complained that these "social contract" achievements were not particularly sustainable, but TRAC seems to have fully honored its social contract commitments.

An evaluation of the corridor by U.S. Agency for International Development (USAID) in 2008 found that the TRAC concession had led to major improvements in corridor highway capacity. The road was by then serving as the main mode connecting Maputo to Gauteng, despite the corridor's historical dependence on rail, although some of this dominance had to do with the delays in rehabilitating the rail line. The USAID study found that tolls on the road were not particularly inexpensive and affected road transport costs significantly, but were still reasonable given the level of reliable service. USAID also found that in terms of transport time to the port, accounting for continuing delays at the border, the toll road performed well. Total transport costs were found to be less for cargo transported by road to Maputo than to Durban (Nathan Associates 2008).

The MDC, anchored by the toll road, is now home to steel mills, petrochemical plants, quarries, mines, smelters, sugar cane and forestry plantations, manufacturing facilities, and tourism facilities. Already by 2002, the corridor had generated over US$5 billion in private sector investments into regional infrastructure development, industrial development, and natural resource exploitation and beneficiation (Thomas 2009).

These various statistics illustrate the key reason why the toll road has been successful over the long term: even though estimates of initial traffic volumes were overly optimistic, those volumes have grown steadily over the last 15 years, making the toll road a strongly commercial venture. Traffic growth rates over this period have been reported at between 5 percent and 7 percent per annum for passenger vehicles, with truck traffic increasing by 10 percent annually. In December 2006, it was estimated that traffic flows ranged between 15,000 vehicles per day (vpd) closer to Mozambique and 30,000 vpd near the Middelberg toll plaza, closer to Gauteng (Hauptfleisch and Marx 2011).

Lack of Progress on Other Corridor PPPs

After the national elections in 1999, virtually all of the original high-level South African political figures and technical experts whose support for the corridor and the toll road had made such a positive impact in 1995 had moved into retirement or new jobs.

By 2003, various private sector entities, particularly those concerned with freight and logistics operations on the corridor, grew concerned about the lack of progress with the remaining key corridor projects. They decided to form a non-profit, multistakeholder company to coordinate, communicate, and facilitate activities in the MDC. In 2004, a collection of South African and Mozambican businesses founded the Maputo Corridor Logistics Initiative (MCLI), with an office opened in Nelspruit, a board of directors, and a membership fee structure to ensure some sustainability. In 2006, the South African DOT joined the MCLI board and became a "founding member." By 2011, MCLI had 170 members. The MCLI's concerns reflected the fact that most of the other key infrastructure projects along the corridor had encountered problems and lost momentum:

The Maputo rail line: In the Framework Agreement signed by the two transport ministers in 1996, the governments agreed to work together to upgrade the Ressano Garcia rail line linking Gauteng to Maputo Port. Following two unsuccessful attempts to concession the railway, which began with a much-publicized signing ceremony in January 2002, the two heads of state agreed in late 2006 that the concession concept should be abandoned. Much of the difficulty in finalizing an agreement seems to have involved the central role in the project given to Spoornet, South Africa's railway parastatal.[6] Spoornet first could not reach agreement on partnership arrangements with a private consortium partner, New Limpopo Bridge Project Investments, and then had difficulties reaching agreement with its Mozambican counterpart, Caminhos de Ferro Moçambique (CFM). It appeared to many observers that Spoornet was unwilling to divert rail traffic to Maputo from the South African ports at Durban and Richards Bay, owned by Spoornet's parent parastatal, Transnet. These suspicions were fuelled by Spoornet's inability or unwillingness to deliver contracted volumes of coal to the Maputo port over the 2002–06 period. The heads of state agreement in 2006 included a stipulation that CFM would downsize, restructure its workforce, assume responsibility for US$70 million rehabilitation of the line, and manage its operation from Maputo to the border. Spoornet agreed to provide rolling stock and facilitate trade volumes, and bulk freight reaching the Maputo port increased under this new arrangement. But questions remain about Spoornet's other investment needs and business priorities. Spoornet seems to have carried on with its policy of limiting rail traffic to Maputo even after the 2006 agreement.

Maputo port: The two governments had also agreed early on regarding the need to use private participation to rehabilitate, develop, and operate the port. The Mozambican government invited tenders in 1997 and signed an agreement with a preferred bidder in 2000. Financial closure was finally reached in April 2003 when the preferred bidder assumed that the rail rehabilitation project was under way. The port (along with an adjacent port facility known as the Matola Port) was concessioned to the Maputo Port Development Company, 51 percent owned by an international consortium led by Mersey Docks Group (UK) and 49 percent owned by the Mozambican government. The contract was for 15 years, after which the concessionaire has an option to continue for another 10 years. After implementation of the port project began, it became clear that the announced agreement on a rail rehabilitation project had fallen through. Lacking cargo that was expected to come via rail, the port concessionaire was unable to pay rental feels for a period and could not declare dividends. In 2006, it was still making a loss. But in 2007, after the rail rehabilitation was finally showing results, the port became profitable as the volumes of bulk cargo reaching the port improved. (The outstanding fees were later repaid.) By mid-2011, about US$225 million had been invested in the two ports, with another US$750 million expected to be invested over the next two decades. In 1970, annual freight throughput at the port was 13.7 million tons, but by the early 1990s that figure had dropped to just over 2 million tons. By the time the concession was signed in 2003, the figure had risen to 5 million tons. By 2011, the throughput had reached 12.6 million tons, with expectations that the figure would double by 2015 (Picanyol 2009).

One-stop border post: The two governments agreed that to maximize the potential of the road and railway, a one-stop border post was needed to facilitate timely cross-border transport of passengers and freight. But it proved difficult to get consensus on the concept, design, and related systems of a new border post because of the large number of stakeholders within and across the two countries. Some incremental improvements were made in border processing, and in June 2006, both governments reconfirmed their agreement to move to a one-stop border post. In 2010, a freight bypass road was opened, effectively providing a one-stop option for freight traffic. Road passenger facilities are still under construction and a rail facility will be considered at a later time. The border post has a significant impact on the use of the road, especially by commercial trucking vehicles. Extensive processing delays have long been a characteristic of this border crossing since 1994. And even just a two-hour border delay on the way to Maputo port significantly improves the attractiveness of the route to Durban from Pretoria in the eyes of shippers. In 2007, DBSA engineers estimated that

400 trucks a night were leaving Gauteng for Maputo, as compared with 2,000 trucks a night leaving for Durban (Copley and Shaw 2007).

Electricity supply to Southern Mozambique: In addition to the toll road, the construction of power transmission lines into Mozambique was one of the few infrastructure rehabilitation projects in the MDC that proceeded on schedule, without major problems, but this project was never envisioned as a PPP. South Africa's electricity generating parastatal, Eskom, and its counterparts in Electricidade de Mocambique (Mozambique electricity; EDM), and Swaziland (the Swaziland Electricity Board) created the Mozambique Transmission Company (Motraco) to coordinate and facilitate electricity supply to Swaziland and southern Mozambique. Financed initially with US$130 million, Motraco successfully managed the construction of two new 400 kilovolt lines from Mpumalanga to Maputo, and the construction of a new substation in Maputo near the Mozal smelter. The investments made possible a secure source of power for Mozal, and also supplied power for various industrial, commercial, and residential purposes in Mozambique and Swaziland.

Supporting Industrial Development

The Mozal aluminum smelter project remains the key anchor industrial investment in the corridor. At an overall cost of US$2 billion, the first phase of the smelter was completed in 2000, producing 250,000 tons of aluminum ingots per year. A second phase was completed in 2003, bringing total production to just over 500,000 tons per year, or about 2 percent of the world's annual consumption. A third phase is in development, which would bring about another 50 percent in production to almost 750,000 tons per year. According to the International Development Association (IDA), Mozal added more than 10 percent to Mozambique's GDP in 2001; in its first five years, it generated more than US$300 million in foreign exchange earnings for the country, and created 15,000 jobs during the first two phases of construction (IDA 2007).

Other industrial projects have moved ahead as well. The 630 hectare Beluluane Industrial Park has been created adjacent to the Mozal smelter and is now home to 20 companies with linkages to Mozal. The Pande/Temane Natural Gas project was completed in February 2004, with an investment of US$1.2 billion by South African natural gas parastatal Sasol. The project includes development of the Mozambican gas fields at Temane and Pande, and the construction of an 865 kilometers pipeline to Secunda in Mpumalanga for distribution of gas into the South African market.

Summary of Key Problems and Success Factors

The South African fast-track approach to project preparation led to a number of problems with the N4 PPP project, including the following:

• Lack of robust prebid feasibility studies and weak initial project design
• Shortcuts in project procurement, particularly regarding prequalification of bidders

- Difficulties in comparing bids due to different feasibility assessments and design assumptions used
- Weak environmental (and other) safeguards
- Lack of stakeholder consultation
- Lack of involvement by local governments
- Lack of prior legal-regulatory development in Mozambique
- Lack of meaningful project participation by Mozambique and Swaziland
- Absence of a regional dimension to the project in the sense of any involvement by SADC
- Lack of synergistic development of complementary MDC infrastructure projects (especially the rail, border post projects), which might have benefited from a more coordinated project development approach

The fast-track approach, combined with a concession structure dominated by construction companies probably led to, or at least exacerbated, additional problems that could have affected the long-term commercial viability of the project:

- Overly optimistic traffic forecasts
- Failure to anticipate resistance to tolls
- Inadequate construction quality control—many latent defects in construction
- Failure to anticipate road safety issues
- Failure to identify pavement thickness issues
- Failure to identify the implications of a complete absence of government regulations on truck loading

Finally, the project also displays an unusually strong array of success factors that seem to be responsible for the project's success and sustainability, despite shortcomings in preparation:

- Adequate traffic volumes, even before the concession was signed
- Strong prospects for traffic growth, based on government plans to develop 150 projects along the corridor
- Key commercial anchor projects, such as Mozal, with good prospects for successful implementation
- Adequately maintained existing road, most of it in South Africa, which could be tolled almost immediately
- Exceptionally strong high-level political support
- In-house technical capacity, leadership, and commitment on the South African side, especially in DOT
- A 10-year history of trade and transport activity along the corridor
- The fast-track development approach, while causing problems, also helped avoid crippling debates about tolling and PPPs, and other potential causes of project delays

Key Questions in Defining a Role for RECs in Regional PPPs

The N4 toll road project raises a number of questions about regional PPP projects in Sub-Saharan Africa and the possible roles that RECs might play in helping such projects reach financial closure:

1. *Would the N4 have been more successful if it had been more inclusive, more regional, in nature?* The project certainly would have avoided criticism (from inside and outside the South African government) that DOT was moving too fast and not bringing along other stakeholders. Among other things, a stronger regional dimension for the project would have necessitated more capacity building for Mozambique, which probably would have accelerated that country's pipeline of PPP projects, and might have helped facilitate Mozambique's ability to add value on the other infrastructure PPPs along the corridor. Assuming that SADC had expertise and funding, direct involvement in the project by the REC could have helped DOT's engineers understand the PPP dimensions of their project a bit better. With SADC funding, a more thorough, deliberate approach to preparation, safeguards, consultations, and so on might have been possible. If nothing else, SADC involvement probably would have helped other REC members better understand how the PPP mechanism worked.

2. *If the N4 were being developed today, are there ways in which an REC could add value to the project, with upstream preparation, legal-regulatory assessments, or other contributions?* If the project were being done today, it could look very different. Most likely it would require more government support, possibly in the form of minimum revenue or traffic guarantees, availability payments, shadow tolls, partial risk guarantees, or grants. These kinds of PPPs have become more sophisticated since the Asian crisis, and governments need more technical PPP capacity to do them, along with more funding for preparation, regulatory assessments and (if necessary) harmonization, and viability gap grants (and other kinds of subsidies). For cross-border projects, someone needs to ensure that basic preparation activities, like feasibility studies in different participating countries, cover the same issues and speak the same language. RECs or other regional entities could theoretically provide funding for this kind of work and manage its use in connection with regional PPP projects.

Notes

1. This is a finding of the World Bank—PPIAF, Private Participation in Infrastructure (PPI) Project Database.

2. Government procurement rules at the time required a contract to be finalized within six months of appointing a preferred bidder, or negotiations would have to begin with the second-ranked bidder.

3. In retrospect, the N4 contract involved remarkably little government support. As the contract was signed, the Asian financial crisis was beginning to sweep across the developing world and it took 10 years for PPPs to regain the investment levels of 1997. When the toll road PPP market had recovered by about 2005, the projects no longer looked like the N4. They were backed with minimum traffic or revenue guarantees, availability payments, shadow tolls, PRGs, and grants. The N4 was one of the few pre-1997 "classic" toll road PPPs to survive the Asian crisis (Queiroz and Izaguirre 2008).

4. The main piece of Mozambican legislation governing private toll roads is Decree No. 31/96 of July 16.

5. In reality of course, these demands that private partners shoulder all the costs associated with contract mistakes or changes were completely unrealistic. The resulting contracts were extremely fragile because they were completely inflexible. No concessionaire would go into bankruptcy because of a bidding mistake. Concessionaires simply defaulted on contract obligations, let the agreements terminate prematurely, and then tried to take advantage of termination clauses that usually guaranteed government take-over of debt obligations and sometimes equity repayment.

6. Spoornet is now known as Transnet Freight Rail.

West African Gas Pipeline Case

Introduction

The West African Gas Pipeline (WAGP) is a 680 kilometer regional high-pressure gas transmission system. It was built to export gas from the gas reserves in Nigeria's Escravos region of the Niger Delta area to Ghana, Benin, and Togo. The WAGP is the first such pipeline to be installed in Sub-Saharan Africa. It is also one of the largest fossil fuel projects undertaken in Africa.

Inception of the WAGP dates back to 1982, when its development was proposed by the Economic Community of West African States (ECOWAS). The governments of Nigeria, Benin, Togo, and Ghana signed a Heads of Agreement in 1995 and undertook the feasibility study for the project in 1999. A memorandum of understanding was signed by the participating countries in the second half of 1995 and an intergovernmental agreement was signed in early 2000. The project implementation agreement was signed in 2003. The pipeline is owned and operated by the West African Gas Pipeline Company (WAGPCo), a special purpose vehicle incorporated in Bermuda for the development of the pipeline. It is led by Chevron, which has a working interest of 36.7 percent. The shareholders of the WAGPCo project company are presented in table E.1:

The pipeline was completed at a cost of US$900 million, approximately US$310 million (or 52 percent) more than originally estimated. It was put into commercial

Table E.1 Ownership of WAGPCo

Shareholder	% Ownership
Chevron	36.7
Nigerian National Petroleum Corporation	25.0
Royal Dutch Shell	18.0
Volta River Authority (Takoradi Power Company Ltd.)	16.3
SoToGaz[a]	2.0
SoBeGaz	2.0

Source: World Bank.
a. Société Togolaise de Gaz (Togolese Gas Company; SoToGaz) and Société Beninoise de Gaz (Beninese Gas Company; SoBeGaz) are public oil companies in Togo and Benin, respectively.

operation in March 2011. It has an initial capacity of 160 MMBtu/day, expandable to 474 MMBtu/day. The technical specifications of the WAGP are as follows:

- 680 kilometers of mainly 20" pipeline from Nigeria to Ghana; delivery points in Benin, Togo, and Ghana (8", 10", and 18" lateral lines)
- Compressor station on Lagos Beach: 2 × 12,500 HP (one standby) in Phase 1
- Expansion stages: initial capacity 160 MMBtu/day
- Final capacity of 474 MMBtu/day; that is, potential for 2,500–3,000 mega-watts on combined cycle power plants)
- Expansion by increasing compression capacity
- Initially, 85 percent of gas to power plants; 15 percent to heat using industries

The 569 kilometers long offshore section runs parallel to the coastline, approximately 15–20 kilometers offshore, in water depths of between 30 and 75 meters (map E.1).

Map E.1 Sections of the West African Gas Pipeline

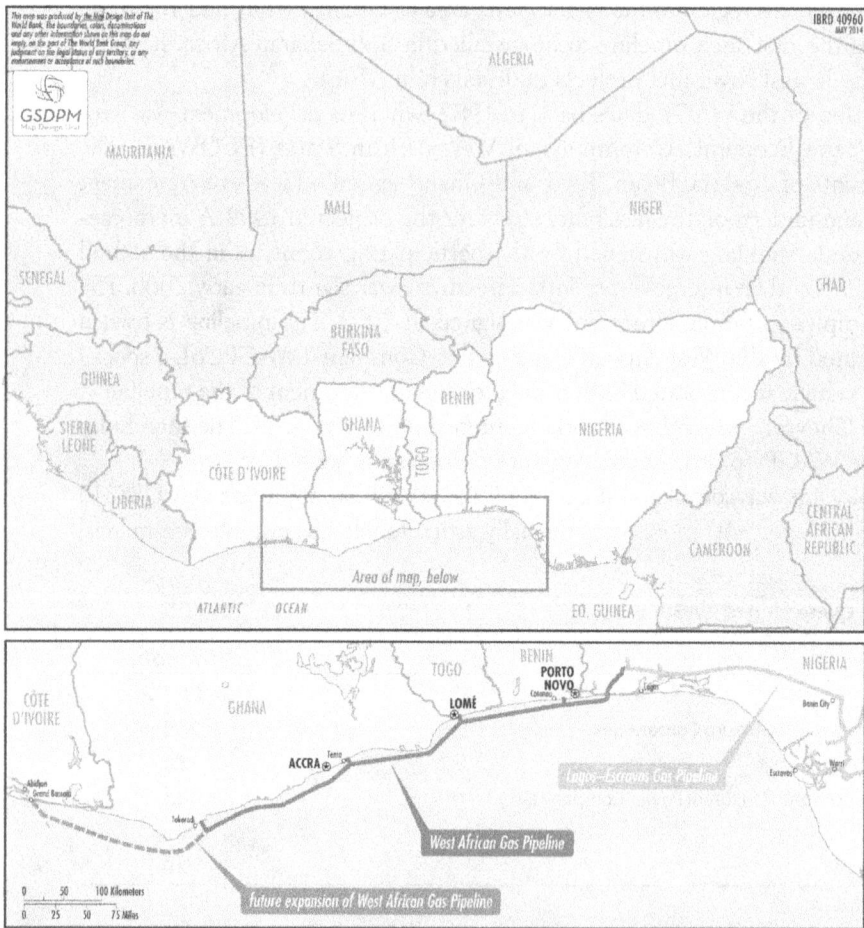

Source: World Bank.

At three locations, connections are made from the main offshore trunk into 8" or more lateral spurs, which will transport gas to delivery points at or near Cotonou (Benin), Lomé (Togo), and Tema (Ghana). The final terminal is at the Takoradi Power Stations (Ghana).

Background

The WAGP was a regional project conceived as an initiative of the Economic Community of West African States (ECOWAS) to establish a West African Power Pool (WAPP). The motivation for WAGP is best understood in the context of the WAPP. ECOWAS is a regional economic community of 15 member states founded in 1975. Its members are Benin, Cape Verde, Cote d'Ivoire, Gambia, Ghana, Guinea, Guinea Bissau, Liberia, Mali, Niger, Nigeria, Senegal, Sierra Leone, and Togo. With about 306 million people and a gross domestic product (GDP) of US$316 billion in 2011, ECOWAS accounts for 4.5 percent of the world's population but only 0.5 percent of the world's GDP. Yet the region has good prospects for economic growth, given its mineral resources, a strategic location that facilitates trade, and a sizable amount of arable land.

Despite the region's large energy endowment, its per capita electricity consumption is among the lowest in the world. Prior to the WAGP project, each country in the region had made efforts to achieve energy self-sufficiency. However, the costs of power system expansion had made it difficult for each country to pursue energy development on its own. The reliance on hydro-based power systems and lack of adequate transmission infrastructure (within and between national power systems) did not provide sufficient security of supply in the region. ECOWAS members concluded that a regional solution would help to provide improved energy security. The approach to such a regional solution would be a pooling mechanism (WAPP) to help integrate national power system operations into a unified regional electricity market to assure the region with a stable and reliable electricity supply at affordable cost. The two systems, WAGP and WAPP, would create the foundation for a regional energy market and cross-border exchange between national utilities.

The WAPP was created by Decision A/DEC.5/12/99 during the 22nd Summit of the Authority of ECOWAS Heads of State and Government in 1999 to address the issue of power supply deficiency within West Africa. The vision of WAPP is to integrate national power system operations into a unified regional electricity market, with the expectation that such a mechanism will, over the medium to long term, assure the citizens of ECOWAS Member States a stable and reliable electricity supply at affordable costs. The following objectives have been declared for the WAPP:

- Formalize an official and extended collaboration in the region to develop power generation and transmission facilities, thus enhancing power supply and strengthening power security within the subregion.
- Improve the reliability of power systems and quality of power supply in the region as a whole.
- Minimize the operating cost of networks.

- Increase investments needed for power grid expansion in the region, with emphasis on the implementation of cross-border projects.
- Create an attractive environment for investments to facilitate the funding of power generation and transmission facilities.
- Create common operating standards and rules in the sector.
- Create a transparent and reliable mechanism for the swift settlement of power trade transactions.
- Increase the overall level of power supply in the region through the implementation of priority generation and transmission projects that will serve as the foundation for economic development and the extension of cheaper electricity to a greater number of consumers.

While the conception of the WAGP predated the formalization of the WAPP, it is clear that the emergence of WAPP as the broad vision of the ECOWAS energy strategy reinforced the importance of the WAGP and strengthened the commitment of the contracting states (Nigeria, Ghana, Benin, and Togo) and the wider ECOWAS membership to the WAGP.

Project Objectives

The WAGP was set up to supply Nigerian gas to Benin, Togo, and Ghana for use in power generation. This would ultimately replace more expensive fuel oil or diesel that was being used for power generation in the region. Gas would be delivered to the Volta River Authority in Ghana for electricity generation, while the Société Beninois de Gas (Beninese Gas Company, SoBeGaz) of the Republic of Benin and Société Togolais de Gas (Togolese Gas Company, SoToGaz) of the Republic of Togo would buy part of the gas for use in their power and industrial plants. The ancillary benefits included:

- New markets for Nigerian gas: WAGP would provide Nigeria and foreign investors in Nigeria an additional commercial market for natural gas. It would also provide an opportunity to reduce wasteful gas flaring associated with local oil production
- Access to cleaner and cheaper fuel and greater energy security for Benin, Togo, and Ghana
- ECOWAS regional economic integration
- A precedent for other cross-border/regional projects

The Political Context

A number of political and governance challenges were faced by the participating countries. Among the four countries involved, two are French speaking and two are English speaking. The four countries also have different legal systems. The French-speaking countries, Benin and Togo, are civil law countries, while Ghana and Nigeria are common law countries. With the exception of Nigeria, the remaining three countries did not have any pipeline experience and the investments involved were substantial for the three smaller countries. The four countries were also at various stages in their political development. In the years preceding the agreements on the WAGP, the state of political play within the countries involved was as follows:

1. **Ghana:** After several military regimes interspersed with short-lived constitutional regimes and an 11-year spell of military government (1981–92), a new constitution was adopted in 1992. On the eve of the WAGP Treaty, Ghana had had 11 years of continuous parliamentary democracy.
2. **Nigeria:** Much like Ghana, Nigeria had since independence experienced several military interventions and a civil war before the current constitution came into force in 1999. Starting from 1999, regular parliamentary elections have been held every four years. Unlike Ghana, the same political party has been in office since 1999. On the eve of the 2003 WAGP Treaty, Nigeria had experienced only four years of uninterrupted parliamentary democracy.
3. **Togo:** Since 1967, Togo had been ruled by President Eyadema under one-party rule. Although an opposition existed, it was so weak that for all practical purposes, Togo was under one-man rule until Eyadema died in 2005.
4. **Benin:** In 1990, a new democratic constitution was adopted. Benin was the first African country to effectively transition from a dictatorship to a pluralistic political system. Since then, there has been a succession of elections, although President Mathieu Kéréko ruled for most of the period leading up to the WAGP Treaty.

Negotiations between countries with very different political experiences and orientation were challenging. However, all four countries were members of ECOWAS and were committed to its objectives. President Eyadema of Togo had served twice as Chairman of ECOWAS (1977/78 and 1999). Ghana's President John Agyekum Kufuor was the Chairman of ECOWAS during 2003–05, the critical years during which the key agreements between the four countries were negotiated and signed. The common commitment to ECOWAS was clearly instrumental in the successful conclusion of the agreements.

Harmonizing the Enabling Environment

The legal, political, and institutional differences between the contracting countries called for special measures to improve the enabling environment. It was important to establish across all four countries a harmonized comprehensive fiscal, regulatory, legal, and investment regime. As the treaty governing the pipeline was being negotiated, the themes that would guide the development of a harmonized regime for the entire ECOWAS region were being encoded in the ECOWAS Energy Protocol. In addition, the following mechanisms were used to achieve harmonization specifically for the WAGP:

- The WAGP Treaty
- International Project Agreement (IPA)
- Enabling legislation passed in all countries

ECOWAS Energy Protocol

The ECOWAS Energy Protocol, signed by ECOWAS Heads of States and Governments in December 2003,[1] established a legal framework for cooperation in the energy sector (see box E.1). The ECOWAS Energy Protocol was modeled on the European Energy Charter with objectives that included ensuring free trade of energy, equipment, products, and services related to energy among member states and defining nondiscriminatory rules for regulated trade activity and dispute resolution.

WAGP Treaty

The WAGP Treaty was signed in January 2003. The WAGP Authority was established as a regulatory authority with functions that include the following:

- Compliance by WAGPCo with its obligations under the IPA
- Approve pipeline design and construction plans
- Negotiate and agree with WAGPCo the licenses and access code
- Negotiate and agree upon the appointment of a third-party operator of the pipeline system
- Negotiate and agree on any expansion plans
- Coordinate the administration of the fiscal laws applying to the WAGP-related activities

---

Box E.1 Main Provisions of the ECOWAS Energy Protocol

Art 6: Open access to power generation and transmission facilities…

Art 7: Freedom of transit without discrimination—even in case of dispute, transit must be guaranteed until the conclusion of the dispute resolution…

Art 9: Access to national capital market on a basis no less favorable than that for the national companies…

Art 11: Permit investors to employ any key personnel they want regardless of nationality and citizenship…

Art 12: "No less favorable treatment" principle is applicable to restitution, indemnification, compensation or other settlement following a war or armed conflict, state of national emergency, civil disturbance, or other similar events…

Art 13: Nationalization or expropriation is forbidden in the area, except when it is carried out of public interest… The amount of compensation is based on market value before the decision and includes interest for any payment delay…

Art 14: Guarantee the freedom of transfer, into and out of the area without delay and in a freely convertible currency, of capital and payments related to the investment activity…

Art 19: Each Contracting Party shall strive to minimize in an economically efficient manner harmful environmental impact…

- Negotiate and agree with WAGPCo on changes in tariff methodology
- Use best efforts to ensure that each state complies with the IPA and applicable enabling legislation.

In addition, the Treaty:

- Established bodies for legal and fiscal appeals
- Reinforced a joint commitment to implement the IPA
- Provided a framework for the sharing of fiscal commitments/revenues among countries
- Disallowed transit royalties and thereby eliminated unnecessary cost additions and administrative process with countries getting their income from taxes on profits

International Project Agreement

The International Project Agreement (IPA) was signed by the four project countries and WAGPCo in May 2003. The key provisions of the IPA covered the following:

- Establishment of the commercial and regulatory terms of the WAGP business
- Adoption of a comprehensive and harmonized investment regime to enable WAGPCo to operate as a single business entity across the four countries
- Licensing of WAGPCo to build, own, operate, and maintain the pipeline system
- Establishment of tariff methodology principles
- Confirmation of the pipeline development plan outline
- Establishment of pipeline access code principles
- Provision of an Environmental Impact Assessment and Management Plan
- Use of a dispute resolution mechanism for technical and other disputes

Control of the transportation tariff levels was an important issue for all four states and the sponsors. The states were adamant that there would be some form of regulation of transportation tariffs, but they were flexible as to exactly how this would occur. The states also wanted the project company to take some risk on market growth by creating spare capacity in the pipeline. The sponsors accepted this, but were dubious about forecasts for market growth and insisted that the tariffs had to provide a reasonable return regardless of the growth realized and a higher return if significant growth was eventually realized.

The tariff methodology set out in the IPA provides a floor rate of return to the company but shares the benefits of growth in the market with all shippers. Thus, as the market grows, tariffs decline in real terms. The tariff methodology is designed so that WAGPCo will achieve its expected rate of return over about 20 years. It will achieve a lower return if the market growth is less than forecast, but this is still a return which the sponsors were prepared to accept on the basis that they were taking some risk on market growth. WAGP tariff charges are calculated using a bottom-up approach to yield a 12 percent rate of return on foundation contracted capacity of 134 millions of cubic feet per day (MMcfd) and a 15 percent rate of return for additional customers as volume grows (up to 450 MMcfd) in the upcoming years calculated on the basis of a 20-year project lifetime for their investment.

Enabling Legislation

The Treaty and the IPA provided for a harmonized fiscal and regulatory framework for cross-border WAGP construction and operations. The key provisions of the WAGP Treaty and the IPA were enacted by the legislatures of the contracting countries in the following enabling laws:

- Uniform Law on the Legal and Fiscal Regime applicable in Benin to the West African Gas Pipeline
- West African Gas Pipeline Act 2004, Ghana
- West African Gas Pipeline Act 2005, Nigeria
- Law on the Legal and Fiscal Regime applicable in the Togolese Republic to the West African Gas Pipeline

Fiscal Regime

The harmonized fiscal regime applied across the entire region to all WAGP activity. The key elements were as follows:

- A 35 percent income tax rate
- Taxable income is determined after deducting clearly defined allowable expenses and reliefs from assessable income; interest expense is limited to a debt:equity cap of 70:30
- 25 percient reducing balance method of depreciation
- A five-year tax holiday
- Nine-year tax loss carry-forward
- No import/customs duties or value added tax (VAT) on import of capital goods
- No transit royalties
- Single tax filing and country assessment process; each WAGP company produces identical returns for each state
- The tax authorities in the states jointly review the returns in conjunction with the WAGP Authority and prepare a single combined assessment on the basis of the information contained in the returns. The WAGP Authority on behalf of the tax authority in each state issues the combined assessment to the WAGP company concerned within 90 days of the filing date
- Minor taxes aggregated and capped
- Exchange control rules harmonized

An important aspect of the fiscal regime was tax sharing between countries. Income tax was shared in proportion to distance or investment amount in states and reserved capacity by state on the basis of the following formula:

$$APs\ (\%) = 45 \times ((LS \div LT) + (RCS \div RCT)) + 2.5$$

where:

APs = apportionment percentage for a state
LS = length in state
LT = total length of pipeline
RCS = reserved capacity by state
RCT = total reserved capacity

The formula is also valid for sharing of project costs incurred collectively by the states.

Tendering Process and Contract Award

Schedule 11 of the IPA specifies the bidding procedures that apply to all procurement by WAGPCo in respect of major contracts. It is stated that the objective of the bidding procedures is to establish the minimum standards that obtain the greatest value for all stakeholders considering safety, quality, cost, schedule, and balanced risk allocation. Consistent with this objective, the overall goals of contracting efforts shall be in conformity with international procurement standards and will meet the following guiding principles:

1. Maintain fully transparent, confidential, and fair contracting and procurement practices, avoiding even the appearance of conflicts of interest
2. Maintain a competitive environment, balancing scope definition, cost, schedule, risk, and administrative burden, resulting in selection of the best qualified contractors on a worldwide basis
3. Maximize the opportunities for local contractors and suppliers to participate in the project, subject to the requirements of the IPA
4. Maximize contracted resources, focused on creating value for the shareholders
5. Achieve the lowest Weighted Average Tariff
6. Maintain full compliance with prevailing governmental regulations in the states.

All contracts are expected to contain provisions requiring the parties thereto to comply with the provisions of the IPA and all applicable local laws, treaties, and regulations of each state. In addition, all contracts are to contain provisions requiring the parties to comply with the World Trade Organization, the United States Foreign Corrupt Practices Act, the United Kingdom Anti-Bribery Legislation, and the Organisation for Economic Co-operation and Development (OECD) Convention on Combating Bribery of Foreign Public Officials in International Business Transactions.

Local content is an evaluation point of both the prequalification and the tender evaluation process. Contractors are required as part of their tender submittals to include specific local content utilization plans. Comprehensive prescriptions are provided for evaluation criteria and procedures for all aspects of procurement including the following:

- Prequalification
- Preparation of tender documents
- Technical and financial evaluations
- Preparation of contract documents
- Contract administration and changes
- Contractor reporting requirements
- Contractor invoicing
- Insurance and bonding requirements
- Contractor and vendor dispute resolution and arbitration
- Audits

Environmental and Social Issues

The project was subject to Environmental and Social Impact Assessments (EIAs), including public consultation. Detailed environmental management plans (EMP) and resettlement action plans (RAP) were developed to provide mitigation, compensation, and monitoring requirements for the project. The conclusion of the assessment was that no potentially high severity impacts would remain after the planned mitigation measures were applied.

The Project Value Chain and Contractual Basis

It was agreed from the outset that the pipeline would operate solely as a gas transporter, not as a marketer of gas. Therefore, the regulation of pricing was restricted only to the transportation tariffs. As WAGPCo does not sell gas, it has no control over the pricing of the gas itself and recovers its investment costs through tariff charges. The players along the value chain are:

1. *N-Gas Limited:* A newly formed entity owned by the Nigerian National Petroleum Corporation (NNPC) (62.35 percent), ChevronTexaco N-Gas Limited (20 percent), and Shell Overseas Holdings Limited (17.65 percent). N-GAS is the supplier of the natural gas from the Escravos-Lagos gas pipeline, which transports natural gas from the main source, the Escravos gas field operated by Chevron in the Niger Delta region of Nigeria. N-Gas also acts as the seller of the gas, having established off-take agreements with the state-owned electricity companies of Benin (Communaute Electrique du Benin, CEB) and Ghana (Volta River Authority, VRA)

2. *Nigerian Gas Company (NGC):* A wholly owned subsidiary of NNPC, under contract from N-Gas, transports natural gas from its sources in Nigeria to a terminal near Lagos over the existing Escravos-Lagos Pipeline System (ELPS)

3. **West African Gas Pipeline Company Limited (WAGPCo):** It is the transporter of gas. WAGPCo recovers its investments and its operating costs through transportation tariff charges under its Gas Transportation Agreements (GTAs) with N-Gas and other future shippers. The system, which spans across four countries, generates revenue streams from the entire pipeline, rather than from activities in individual countries

4. **The Foundation Customers (Offtakers):** The pipeline was financed based on amounts contracted upfront with the core customers, namely VRA and CEB.

The contractual foundations of the project were based on the value chain shown in figure E.1:

1. The producers will sell natural gas to N-Gas under long-term Gas Purchase Agreements.
2. N-Gas will engage the transporters to move the gas under long-term GTAs.
3. N-Gas will sell the gas to the Foundation Customers under long-term Gas Sales Agreements.

Estimated Project Costs and Financing

The project was initially estimated at US$590 million. Additional compression-related costs were estimated at US$110 million over 20 years, which will be needed if the capacity requirement grows from the initial estimate of 160 MMBtu/day to the demand target of 474,000 MMBtu/day. The participants in the project were quite different in terms of funding capability. A decision needed to be made at an early stage whether project financing would be used. Interestingly, although the project has solid project finance characteristics, project finance in the form of nonrecourse debt was not used. Rather, the sponsors agreed that they would fund the initial development entirely with equity capital.

Figure E.1 The Project Value Chain

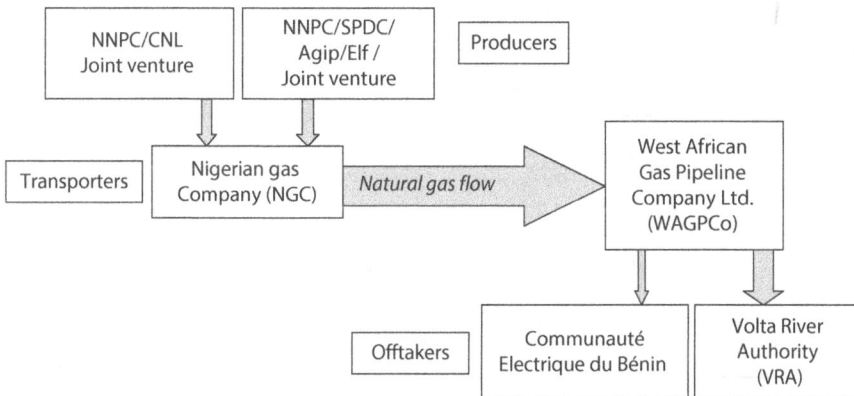

Source: World Bank.
Note: NNPC = Nigerian National Petroleum Corporation; CNL = Chevron Nigeria Limited; SPDC = Shell Petroleum Development Corporation of Nigeria Limited.

The initial capital investment of pipeline construction cost was financed mainly through direct equity, cash contributions, and shareholder loans to WAGPCo from the sponsors. The decision not resort to debt financing for this project was made following a comprehensive review of the possibilities for project financing, principally on the grounds of cost, speed, and efficiency.

There were three main reasons for not using the standard project finance model. First, the cost of debt service was estimated around 14.5 percent. With agreed tariff charges set to yield a 12–15 percent rate of return, this cost level of debt service was considered unacceptable. A second reason for not seeking project finance even if the cost of debt service was acceptable was the disproportional credit ratings among the sponsors (that is, Chevron and Shell—highly creditworthy versus the remaining sponsors). As a consequence, lenders would require creditworthy sponsors to guarantee the less creditworthy sponsors to enable access to debt finance and as such it was not considered a good idea by the more creditworthy sponsors. Finally, even if all the above inhibiting factors were mitigated, the project financing arrangements were likely to require considerable time, while the consortium wanted to develop the project as soon as possible.

The initial US$590 million was financed through direct equity and shareholder loans to WAGPCo from the sponsors (table E.2). The shareholder loans were provided by the sponsors for a maturity of 22 years at an interest rate of 10 percent per annum. Subsequent compression-related capital expenditures were expected to be financed by cash flow from operations. WAGPCo's investments were to be recovered through gas transportation charges under its GTAs with N-Gas and other future shippers.

The pipeline was completed at a cost of US$900 million, approximately US$310 million (or 52 percent) more than originally estimated. The additional financing was provided in the form of equity by the sponsors in the same proportions as the initial equity contributions. The United States Agency for International Development (USAID) also supported the project by providing US$1.6 million in technical assistance.

Table E.2 Financing Sources

	Equity (US$ millions)	Shareholder loans (US$ millions)	Total	Percent
Government of Ghana	28.8	67.3	96.1	16.3
NNPC	44.2	103.2	147.4	25.0
CNL	64.9	151.5	216.4	36.7
SPDC	31.8	74.3	106.1	18.0
SoBeGaz	3.5	8.3	11.8	2.0
SoToGaz	3.5	8.3	11.8	2.0
Total	176.7	412.9	589.6	100.0

Source: World Bank.
Note: NNPC = Nigerian National Petroleum Corporation; SoBeGaz = Société Beninoise de Gaz (Beninese Gas Company) S.A.; SoToGaz = Société Togolaise de Gaz (Togolese Gas Company) S.A.

Project Risk Mitigation

Although project finance was not used, project financing techniques were used to lend credit support to the gas purchase obligations, which was essential to give the sponsors the comfort to proceed. Due to the high political and commercial risk involved in the project, the sponsors demanded guarantees from multilateral lending agencies for risk mitigation for the project to proceed.

The project agreements were designed to allocate risks among the parties. Generally, the private sector participants took the construction- and operations-related risks, while the public sector took the payment risks under the Foundation Customers' Gas Sales Agreements (GSAs), which were on a take-or-pay basis in US dollars. Events of *force majeure* were shared among the parties. However, default by the producers in delivering gas in Nigeria would result in liquidated damages to the Foundation Customers.

Figure E.2 presents the risk guarantee instruments structured for the WAGP project. A major issue for the sponsors was the creditworthiness of the payment obligations of the buyers, on the faith of which an investment decision was to be

Figure E.2 WAGP Risk Mitigation Structures

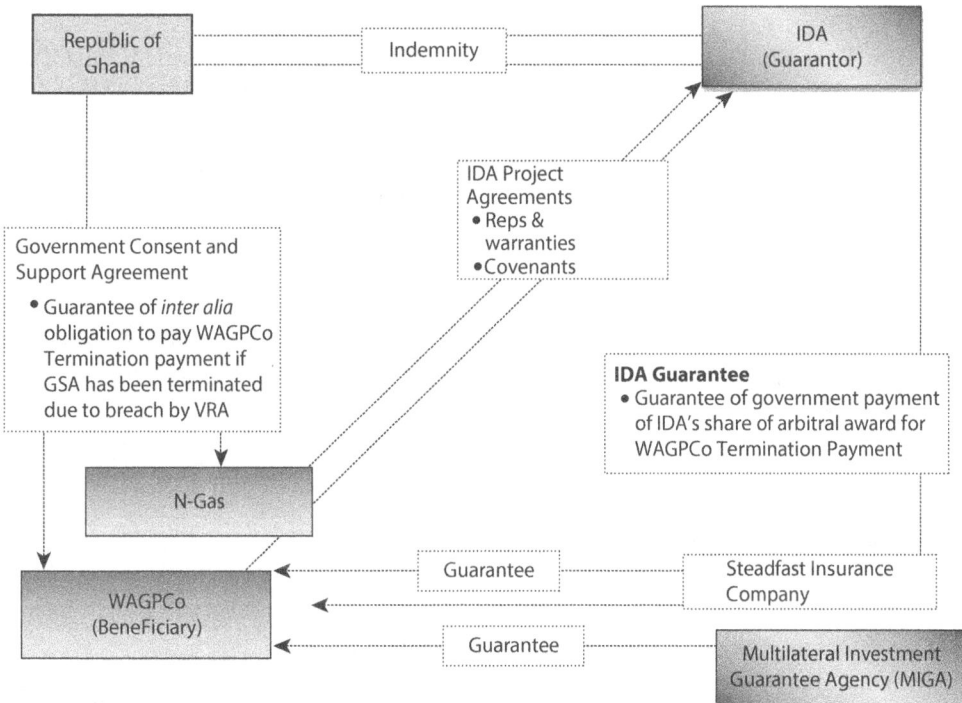

Source: World Bank.
Note: IDA = International Development Association; GSA = Gas Sales Agreement; VRA = Volta River Authority; WAGPCo = West African Gas Pipeline Company.

made. The position of the sponsors was that without some underlying creditworthiness or credit support for the revenue stream, investment could not proceed. The key project risk was payment risk associated with the offtake by the VRA of Ghana, and it was necessary to devise a risk mitigation solution. The basic solution was a Government Consent and Support Agreement backing the obligation. This was further backed by a "triple play" Political Risk Insurance (PRI) offered by:

1. World Bank/IDA Partial Risk Guarantee
2. Multilateral Investment Guarantee Agency (MIGA)
3. Private Sector/Overseas Private Investment Corporation (OPIC) (Zurich Emerging Market Solutions) reinsured by OPIC.

Table E.3 summarizes the components of the PRI instruments.

In November 2004, the World Bank approved two guarantees worth a total of US$125 million for the construction of the project. These two guarantees included US$50 million and US$75 million from the World Bank's International Development Association (IDA) and Multilateral Investment Guarantee Agency (MIGA), respectively. The IDA Guarantee was needed to support the following key project agreements:

- *Takoradi Gas Sales Agreement* (Takoradi GSA) between the VRA and N-Gas, providing for the sales by N-Gas and purchase by VRA of up to 120 MMscf/day of gas on a take-or-pay or ship-or-pay basis
- *Takoradi Gas Transportation Agreement* (Takoradi GTA) between WAGPCo and N-Gas for the gas being sold by N-Gas under the Takoradi GSA
- *VRA Direct Agreement* among VRA, WAGPCo, and N-Gas, whereby N-Gas assigns to WAGPCo (as security for N-Gas's payment obligations to WAGPCo under the Takoradi GTA) the component of the VRA termination payment and arrears owing to N-Gas under the Takoradi GSA corresponding to the same component payable to WAGPCo by N-Gas under the Takoradi GSA and the VRA Direct Agreement
- *Government Consent and Support Agreement* (GCSA), under which Ghana, in compliance with its undertaking under the IPA, irrevocably and unconditionally guarantees to N-Gas and WAGPCo the performance obligations of VRA under the Takoradi GSA and VRA Direct Agreement.

Figure E.3 is a diagrammatic representation of the project structure. indicating all project stakeholders and the web of agreements and contracts that constituted the project.

Implementation and Contract Management

The West African Gas Pipeline Authority ("WAGP Authority" or "WAGPA") was established pursuant to the WAGP Treaty to serve as the regulatory body for the WAGP. In addition, WAGPA has facilitation and representation functions

Table E.3 Political Risk Insurance Instruments

Agency	Amount	Terms
Multilateral Investment Guarantee Agency (MIGA, World Bank)	US$75 million political risk insurance (PRI) up to 20 years	Provides protection to project investment funds (whether acquired through loans, equity, or other forms) against a number of risks such as currency transfer restrictions, inconvertibility, expropriation, war and civil disturbances, and breach of contract.
International Development Association (IDA, World Bank)	US$50 million partial risk guarantee for 22 years	Can be used to cover payment defaults from Volta River Authority (VRA). World Bank's indemnity guarantees will be converted into an automatic loan for Ghana under the West African Gas Pipeline (WAGP), should the Government of Ghana fail to pay N-Gas
Steadfast Insurance Company (subsidiary of Zurich Financial Services Group)	US$125 million political risk insurance	Risk guarantee
Overseas Private Investment Corporation (OPIC)	US$45 million	In the form of reinsurance to Steadfast Insurance Company

Source: World Bank.

Figure E.3 WAGP Project Structure

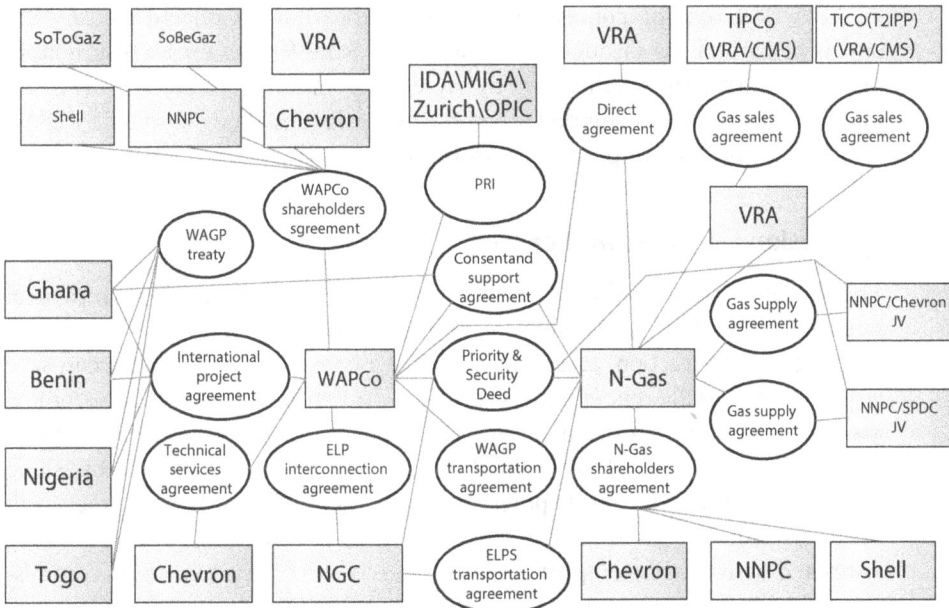

Source: World Bank.
Note: SoToGaz = Société Togolaise de Gaz (Togolese Gas Company) S.A.; SoBeGaz = Société Beninoise de Gaz (Beninese Gas Company) S.A.; VRA = Volta River Authority; NNPC = Nigerian National Petroleum Corporation; PRI = Political Risk Insurance; NGC = Nigerian Gas Company; WAGP = West African Gas Pipeline; ELPS = Escravos-Lagos Pipeline System.

(to take actions and decisions in the name and on behalf of the State Parties). The regulatory functions include inter alia to:

- Monitor compliance by WAGPCo of its obligations under the IPA
- Approve pipeline design and construction
- Negotiate and agree with WAGPCo the licenses and access code and with third-party operators of the pipeline system
- Agree on expansion plans
- Act on behalf of the four states' respective tax authorities
- Negotiate and agree with WAGPCo to changes in tariff methodology
- Use its best efforts to ensure each state complies with the IPA and the enabling legislation.

WAGPA has a Director General who is the Chief Executive Officer. The Director General is a national of a State party to the agreement (henceforth State Party) and is appointed for a term of five years, renewable, by the Committee of Ministers upon the recommendation of the Board of Governors from candidates that are qualified for the position. The Board of Governors is composed of four members appointed for a term of four years. Each member is appointed by the Head of State of the relevant State Party. The Committee of Ministers is composed of the Relevant Minister of each State Party. ECOWAS is invited to attend all meetings of the Committee of Ministers as an observer.

The State Parties are responsible for providing or procuring funding for WAGPA. The funding comes primarily from the WAGPA charge paid by the buyers of natural gas through the WAGP. The State Parties are to ensure at all times, and particularly in the event of any shortfall of funds paid to WAGPA, that the costs in excess are funded from the State Parties' budget so as to allow WAGPA to continue to properly perform its functions.

Conclusions and Lessons Learned

The WAGP is considered an attractive project by its sponsors. The commercial return on investment is favorable and there are regional benefits as well in terms of energy cost reduction. It is estimated that Benin, Togo, and Ghana can save nearly US$500 million in energy costs over a 20-year period, as WAGP-supplied gas is substituted for more expensive fuels in power generation. Ghana estimates that it will save between 15,000 and 20,000 barrels per day of crude oil by taking gas from the WAGP to run its power plants. In addition, the WAGP project will reduce greenhouse gas emissions and air pollutants by cutting down on flaring associated with existing oil production in Nigeria. According to a study commissioned by Chevron, it is estimated that 10,000–20,000 primary sector jobs will be created in the region by the project.

The WAGP has been touted as an example of cooperation and harmonized partnership among countries in the ECOWAS region. It is also seen as a model for public-private cooperation. The WAGP and the WAPP were promoted as New Partnership for Africa's Development (NEPAD)'s priority projects for the ECOWAS region. The project signified the interconnection and sharing of resources to reduce costs, enhance economic growth, alleviate poverty, and ensure environmental protection. There is ample evidence that the participating countries attached tremendous significance to the project. This is seen particularly in the promptness with which the enabling legislations were enacted by the respective parliaments of the participating countries.

Several ancillary benefits have been claimed for the WAGP:

- Accelerated regional economic growth and integration in the ECOWAS region
- Clean, stable, secure, and low-cost energy solutions for the participating countries
- Tax revenues to the four project states estimated at about US$634 million over the project life
- A platform for sharing and exchanging expertise/experience among the project developer, international and local contractors, state agencies, and consultants in natural gas transmission and pipeline system operations
- Reduction of gas flaring and hazardous emissions in the Niger Delta; provision of additional markets for Nigeria's gas; and an increase in the revenue base of Nigeria.

The 1993 revision to the Treaty of Lagos shifted ECOWAS from an organization whose ultimate goal was furthering bilateral cooperation between states to a community that was aimed at bringing about closer social and economic integration. Currency union is a major ambition. Other important objectives include establishing a customs union, a unified tariff regime, and other harmonized economic policies that will allow the member countries to operate as a comprehensive economic bloc. The WAGP and WAPP are manifestations of this renewed regional integration model.

The success of the WAGP is in no small measure due to its linkage with the WAPP and the broad integration agenda of ECOWAS. The role of ECOWAS as the unifying body is reflected in the exemplary cooperation between four contracting states with widely divergent, legal, political, and institutional structures and financial resources. The WAGP also shows that a Regional Economic Community (REC) such as ECOWAS does not necessarily have to own infrastructure to play a supporting role. While the WAGP is owned by the four contracting countries and the private sector, ECOWAS provided political and technical support throughout the process. It is significant that even though the ECOWAS Secretariat is not a contracting party for WAGP, it has observer status on the WAGPA, the regulatory authority of the WAGP.

A major lesson for cross-border infrastructure development is the importance of a harmonized investment and fiscal regime. Through the ECOWAS Energy

Protocol, the building blocks of a harmonized legal and regulatory regime were put in place for the entire ECOWAS region to guide the harmonization agreements for the WAGP. The WAGP demonstrates the potential of RECs to foster infrastructure development through the harmonization of the enabling environment. ECOWAS brought significant benefits at an upstream level (institutional reforms, technical standards, financial mechanisms, and cross-border tariff issues). In the case of the WAGP, the harmonized investment and fiscal regime significantly reduced the transaction cost to the private sector partners and thus increased the attractiveness of the project.

The institutions for the integration of energy markets in the ECOWAS region, the WAPP Secretariat and WAGPA, have identified capacity gaps both at the regional level and for public institutions of member states and private operators working at the country level (ECOWAS 2006). There are opportunities for cooperation with development agencies to support programs that address these skill requirements. The technical assistance support provided by the USAID for the WAGP is an illustration of such cooperation.

Note

1. The Protocol came into force in 2007 following ratification by 10 of the 15 ECOWAS Member States.

EADB: Preliminary Institutional Assessment (as of October 2011)

The East African Development Bank (EADB) is the key regional financial institution in the East African Community (EAC), and has operated continuously, reasonably successfully, with a regional mandate since it was established in 1967. Since 1995, it has approved a total of 549 loans valued at US$763 million. It presently has US$248 million in total assets, US$144 million in net worth (41 percent of total assets), and 110 projects in a loan portfolio valued at US$83 million, of which 14.0 percent (25 projects) are presently nonperforming. Its future prospects for raising additional equity when needed are robust, as it has US$522 million in additional callable capital from its member countries.

It is 88.1 percent owned by its four country members, with Kenya, Tanzania, and Uganda holding equal 26.7 percent shares. Rwanda is in the process of increasing its shareholding to a similar level and Burundi is in the process of applying for membership. African Development Bank (AfDB), German Development Finance Corporation (DEG), and Netherlands Development Finance Company (FMO) hold a combined 11.1 percent share (Class B shares) and an additional 0.75 percent is owned by six private banking entities. In addition to government representatives and an AfDB representative, there are four private directors on the EADB Board of Directors who are prominent businessmen and -women in their respective countries. Despite its public sector ownership, the board has some commercial perspective characteristics. The government representatives (Permanent or Principal Secretaries of Finance) are concerned with the financial ramifications of decision making, while the businessmen have an in-depth understanding of their respective country business environments and a pragmatic perspective on project viability.

While the EADB has recently focused on corporate lending to medium- and smaller-size companies, it has some experience with both regional and infrastructure projects. It has lent a total of US$49.8 million to seven projects within these two categories in recent years. Five of these projects have been fully implemented, all are operating successfully, and all but US$6.7 million has already been repaid.

The EADB has a Fitch credit rating (as of October 2011) of B-, with improvements expected now that the legal case against the EADB in Tanzania has been satisfactorily dismissed. Despite the continued existence of this legal issue, in October 2011, KPMG provided an unqualified opinion on the 2010 accounts.

The EADB has been managed conservatively during the past three years, focusing effectively on cleaning up its portfolio, collecting bad debts, eliminating weaker staff, and building a strong foundation for future expansion and effective performance of a key role it hopes to play in supporting future EAC and East Africa Community Development Fund (EACDF) activities in support of regional and infrastructure finance. The following is a summary of some of the key achievements over this period:

1. The EADB's total assets are significantly lower than they were in 2007 and have grown only 7 percent in the last two and a half years, despite its having adequate access to both local and foreign currency resources. Indeed, its small balance sheet (maximum credit exposure limit set at 15 percent of its definition of net worth) is presently only US$17.5 million.
2. Nonperforming loans (NPLs) have dropped from a high of US$31.6 million (25.8 percent of portfolio) in 2009 to US$11.7 million (14 percent of portfolio) as of September 2011 primarily due to write-offs. Moreover, its loan classification and accounting for bad debt is very conservative, with provisions adding to 88 percent of NPLs as of June 2011.
3. The EADB has taken significant steps to address its biggest weakness, the unsatisfactory quality of its past lending. Most of its NPLs were approved under the direction of a Chief Operating Officer who was later dismissed and the previous Director-General left in 2009. The board, in response to its growing concerns about the portfolio problems, retained KPMG to do a detailed portfolio analysis and tightened controls on new lending considerably. No projects approved in 2008 and thereafter are presently nonperforming. Consequently, 18 of EADB's 25 present NPLs were approved prior to 2007 and the remaining seven NPLs (with a combined US$2.3 million in value) were approved in 2007.
4. The EADB's liquidity position is unusually strong, with cash and bank deposits totaling US$131 million (54 percent of total assets) and it is unlikely to have difficulty in raising additional resources when needed. It has previously floated successful bond issues in Kenya, Tanzania, and Uganda and has reasonable prospects for doing so again in several of its member countries. Callable capital is another source of very long-term local currency. The EADB has had success in getting its member countries to respond satisfactorily to capital calls, but a unanimously positive response may be necessary each time to preserve the equal ownership.
5. Administrative costs, running at an annual rate of 2.9 percent of average total assets in 2011, are well controlled and low for a Development Finance Institution (DFI).

6. While the EADB's present loan portfolio position is sound, its mixed pre-2008 success in lending and, consequently, its record of profitability has been disappointing. While it has been profitable recently, with a combined profit of US$4.8 million over the two and a half years since 2009 (about 1 percent per annum on average assets), it has lost US$17.3 million on an accumulated basis since inception, as a result of providing US$34 million in provisions on nonperforming assets in 2007–08.

The EADB's historical performance, while disappointing in important aspects, has been superior to most other development and government-owned commercial banks in the region. Its present financial condition and, arguably, its near-term prospects for successful financial performance compare very favorably with all other predominantly public sector lending institutions in the EAC.

The EADB is substantially, albeit not fully, protected from weaknesses often associated with public sector governance in lending institutions because of the multicountry nature and significant nongovernmental presence associated with its ownership and board composition.

Nonetheless, the EADB's image in the marketplace and among relevant donors is mixed for a variety of reasons including (i) the need for large write-offs of bad loans prior to 2009; (ii) a generally poor reputation shared by most of Africa's DFIs; (iii) the 88 percent combined government ownership position, which worries some donors; (iv) its small size relative to relevant private commercial institutions in the region; and (v) bad publicity from time to time not adequately balanced by an effective public relations program.

The EADB has 71 staff and full-time consultants, of which 25 (including three lawyers) are operational professionals with significant relevant experience in project preparation, appraisal, and supervision, and the bank is in the process of recruiting four more. Twenty-three of the 25 operational staff has graduate degrees while 14 have Master of Business Administrations (MBAs) or degrees in finance or banking. Four operational staff has economics backgrounds and only three have a technical academic background in engineering or agriculture. Nonetheless, operational staff constraints are a significant issue, especially given the EADB's plans to sharply expand lending of its own funds beginning in 2013.

The EADB has signed a memorandum of understanding (MoU) with the Development Bank of South Africa (DBSA) which has been successful over many years in lending for infrastructure in South Africa. Moreover, it will be receiving relevant ongoing technical assistance from AfDB in the form of a senior consultant on energy and infrastructure projects and has rehired two retired former executives to provide further consulting support in this area.

The EADB's organization and staffing in professional nonoperational support areas appears relatively well positioned to implement a possible role in a Project Preparation Facility (PPF) and/or an EACDF. Its accounting, treasury, and legal functions are competent and highly experienced in dealing with those issues in an East African context. While improvements are likely to be required, it has a meaningful foundation to build on in terms of other future requirements. For example, it has conducted procurement in satisfactory compliance with the requirements of its past suppliers of credit, namely AfDB and European Investment Bank (EIB), and has incorporated country-specific environmental impact and safeguard protection requirement elements that pertain with respect to its past projects.

Recommendations for Improving the EADB

The EADB has been in the business of project preparation and lending for many years, and is viewed by the EAC and its member countries as a key contributor to implementing a regional developmental strategy. If it satisfactorily addresses the remaining weaknesses, it is likely that donors will find the EADB a satisfactory candidate for playing a key role in implementing a regional PPF and, possibly, for hosting an EACDF and, on a parallel basis, a Viability Gap Facility (VGF) if such a fund is formed.

It is recommended that the EADB prepare a satisfactory institutional development program (IDP) to address these weaknesses and better prepare itself for this possible role. The EADB should have the goal of converting itself from its present status as a reasonably good development bank into an excellent one. It is recommended that, inter alia, the following steps be taken to achieve this goal:

1. Approve and implement an IDP satisfactory to its owners and potential donors
2. Conduct an Association of African Development Finance Institutions (AADFI) prudential standards and guidelines compliance review and incorporate reforms, where appropriate, to improve compliance in the IDP
3. Ensure availability of audited accounts for the year ending which, like the 2010 financials, have an unqualified opinion and show continuing satisfactory financial condition and performance
4. Receive a Fitch rating of at least BB
5. Present a satisfactory new five-year business plan, reflecting EADB's desired role in a regional PPP Framework, and with respect to the EACDF and possible VGF and PDF functions.
6. Add one additional Class B share director to represent all Class B shareholders, except AfDB, which should retain its existing seat on the board
7. Prepare a five-year staffing and training program appropriate for effectively performing a role in implementing the EACDF and potential PDF and VGF instruments, possibly inclusive of an expanded MoU with DBSA and incorporating AfDB advisory inputs
8. Conduct a credit risk management study and implement recommendations with the objective of learning from the mistakes of the past and improving policy, procedures, and organizational structure as needed to significantly reduce the risk of repeating them. It is of critical importance that the EADB improve the quality of its future lending
9. Analyze foreign currency risk policies and adjust as necessary to reduce risk as indicated by substantial recent foreign exchange losses
10. Recruit a deal structuring expert.

References

Adam Smith Institute. 2003. "Developing an Infrastructure Regulatory Framework in Kenya." London.

AICD (Africa Infrastructure Country Diagnostics). 2008. "A Time for Transformation." Background Paper #15, Country Annex 2, World Bank, Washington, DC.

Alexander, P., D. W. Burger, G. Esterhuysen, J. J. Smit, and A. Taute. 2004. "Cost and Quality Issues in Road Concession Contracts." Proceedings of the 8th Conference on Asphalt Pavements for Southern Africa, Sun City, South Africa, September 12–16.

Commission on Growth and Development. 2008. "The Growth Report: Strategies for Sustained Growth and Inclusive Development." Published by the International Bank for Reconstruction and Development on behalf of the Commission on Growth and Development, IBRD, Washington, DC.

Copley, Peter, and Andrew Shaw. 2007. "The Evolution of Road Funding in South Africa, within its SADC Context." Paper presented at the International Seminar on Road Financing and Investment, Arusha Tanzania, April 16–20.

CPCS Transcom International. 2009. "East African Railways Master Plan Study." Final Report.

de Beer, Geoffrey. 2011. "Regional Public Goods in Africa: The Maputo Corridor." Paper presented at the Third Africa Policy Seminar on Regional Public Goods in Africa, sponsored by The Collaborative Africa Budget Reform Initiative (CABRI), November.

DOT (Department of Transport). 1996. White Paper on National Transport Policy, Pretoria, August. Downloaded from http://www.info.gov.za/whitepapers/1996/transportpolicy.htm#art 6.

Driver, Amanda, and Joao Gabriel de Barros. 2000. "The Impact of the Maputo Development Corridor on Freight Flows: An initial investigation." Working Paper No. 00/38, Development Policy Research Unit, University of Cape Town, March.

EAC (East African Community). 2011. "EAC Corridor Diagnostic Study of the Northern and Central Corridors of East Africa." Submitted to the Task Coordination Group (TCG) chaired by the EAC, April 2011.

ECOWAS. 2006. "Regional Initiatives to Scale Up Energy Access for Economic and Human Development." ECOWAS Briefing Paper, November. http://www.gfse.at/fileadmin/dam/gfse/gfsepercent206/pdf/CEDEAO_Briefing_paper_for_GFSE_final.pdf.

Fisher, Gregory, and Suman Babbar. 1996. "Private Financing of Toll Roads." RMC Discussion Paper Series 117, Project Finance and Guarantees Group, World Bank, Washington, DC.

Fitch Ratings. 2009. "Latin America Toll Roads: Global Credit Crisis Causes Bumpy Road Ahead." Toll Roads Latin America Special Report, Global Infrastructure and Project Finance, June 17.

Hauptfleisch, Dries, and Hendrik Marx. 2011. "The Potential Impact on Property and Socio-Economic Development Resulting from Road Transport Corridors in Africa: A Case Study." Paper presented at Management and Innovation for a Sustainable built Environment, Amsterdam, The Netherlands, June 20–23.

IDA (International Development Association). 2007. "Encouraging Investments and Economic Growth in Mozambique." Downloaded from the IDA Website: http://web.worldbank.org/WBSITE/EXTERNAL/EXTABOUTUS/IDA.

Interim Co-ordinating Committee. 1996. A Development Perspective: Maputo Development Corridor. Pretoria, Government Printer.

Jourdan, Paul. 1998. "Spatial Development Initiatives (SDIs)—The Official View." *Development Southern Africa* 15 (5, Summer): 717–25.

Leigland, J. 2007. "A PPP Against the Odds." A publication of Public Private Infrastructure Advisory Facility (PPIAF), Nairobi.

Leigland, J. 2010. "Infrastructure Project Preparation in Africa: Costs and Funding Options." Unpublished paper prepared for DFID, London.

Mail and Guardian. 2000. "Huge Road Repair Backlog." Johannesburg, May 15.

Mandela, Nelson. 1996. Speech at the Maputo Development Corridor Investor Conference, South African History Online, May 6. http://www.sahistory.org.za.

Mitchell, Jonathan. 1998. "The Maputo Development Corridor: A Case Study of the SDI Process in Mpumalanga." *Development Southern Africa* 15 (5, Summer): 757–69.

Monsalve, Carolina. 2009. "Private Participation in Transport: Lessons from Recent Experience in Europe and Central Asia." PPIAF Gridline, No. 47, Public-Private Infrastructure Advisory Facility (PPIAF), World Bank, Washington, DC, June.

Nathan Associates. 2008. "Maputo Corridor Summary Report: A Transport Logistics Diagnostic Tool Study." Report prepared for USAID, March.

National Treasury. 2001. National Treasury PPP Manual, Version 1, Pretoria, National Treasury PPP Unit.

Nelsson, A. 2011. "Public Private Partnerships and Management of Strategic Infrastructure in Tanzania 2005 to 2011." World Bank, Washington, DC.

PADECO. 1999. "Asian Toll Road Development Program: Review of Recent Toll Road Experience in Selected Countries and Preliminary Tool Kit for Toll Road Development." Report prepared for the World Bank and the Ministry of Construction, Japan, May.

Picanyol, Clara. 2009. "The Maputo Port Concession." CABRI Dialogue: Ensuring Value for Money in Infrastructure, Case Study 5. Johannesburg: Collaborative Africa Budget Reform Initiative (CABRI).

Queiroz, Cesar, and Ada Karina Izaguirre. 2008. "Worldwide Trends in Private Participation in Roads: Growing Activity, Growing Government Support." PPIAF Gridline, No. 37, Public-Private Infrastructure Advisory Facility (PPIAF), World Bank, Washington, DC, May.

SADC Banking Association. 2003. "Overview of Regulatory and Institutional PPP Environment in Mozambique." Report prepared by Edward Nathan & Friedland and SAL Consultoria e Investimentos, SADC Banking Association, Johannesburg.

Taylor, Ian. 2000. "Public-Private Partnerships: Lessons from the MDC Toll Road." Working Paper No. 00/44, Development Policy Research Unit, University of Cape Town, December.

Thomas, Rosalind. 2009. "Development Corridors and Spatial Development Initiatives in Africa," Downloaded from the MIGA Website, now available at http://www.fdi. net/documents/WorldBank/databases/africa_infrastructure/Thomas_SDI_paper_ lowres.pdf.

UNDP (United Nations Development Programme). 2008. "The N4 Toll Road, South Africa and Mozambique." *Sharing Innovative Experiences* Vol. 15: *Examples of Successful Public-private Partnerships.* New York: United Nations Development Program, South-South Cooperation Unit.

World Bank. 2002. "Kenya Transport Sector Memorandum." World Bank, Washington, DC.

Environmental Benefits Statement

The World Bank is committed to reducing its environmental footprint. In support of this commitment, the Publishing and Knowledge Division leverages electronic publishing options and print-on-demand technology, which is located in regional hubs worldwide. Together, these initiatives enable print runs to be lowered and shipping distances decreased, resulting in reduced paper consumption, chemical use, greenhouse gas emissions, and waste.

The Publishing and Knowledge Division follows the recommended standards for paper use set by the Green Press Initiative. Whenever possible, books are printed on 50 percent to 100 percent postconsumer recycled paper, and at least 50 percent of the fiber in our book paper is either unbleached or bleached using Totally Chlorine Free (TCF), Processed Chlorine Free (PCF), or Enhanced Elemental Chlorine Free (EECF) processes.

More information about the Bank's environmental philosophy can be found at http://crinfo.worldbank.org/wbcrinfo/node/4.